W9-DDO-628

Tending the Heart of Virtue

Tending the Heart of Virtue

How Classic Stories Awaken a Child's Moral Imagination

Vigen Guroian

New York Oxford
Oxford University Press
1998

Oxford University Press

Oxford New York
Athens Auckland Bangkok Bogotá Bombay
Buenos Aires Calcutta Cape Town Dar es Salaam Delhi
Florence Hong Kong Istanbul Karachi
Kuala Lumpur Madras Madrid Melbourne
Mexico City Nairobi Paris Singapore
Taipei Tokyo Toronto Warsaw

and associated companies in
Berlin Ibadan

Published by Oxford University Press, Inc.
198 Madison Avenue, New York, New York 10016

Oxford is a registered trademark of Oxford University Press, Inc.

Library of Congress Cataloging-in-Publication Data
Guroian, Vigen.
Tending the heart of virtue :
how classic stories awaken a child's moral imagination / Vigen Guroian.
p. cm.
Includes bibliographical references and index.
ISBN 0-19-511787-5
1. Children's literature—History and criticism. 2. Virtues in literature. 3. Literature and morals. I. Title.
PN1009.A1G87 1998
809'.89282—DC21 97-45885

1 3 5 7 9 8 6 4 2
Printed in the United States of America
on acid-free paper

To Rafi and Victoria

"All children, except one, grow up."

Peter Pan

I have known since your births
that you would grow up,
although like Peter Pan sometimes I have
wished that you would not.
Now you are no longer the small children
to whom I read bedtime stories.
And I am glad of heart,
because you have both grown up so well.

Contents

Acknowledgments

When I was a child my maternal grandmother, Zabel Keosaian, would come to our home for long stays. That was when my mother, father, brother, and I lived in a small cape cod style home in Stamford, Connecticut. Downstairs there were just four modest rooms, a kitchen, a living room, a small parlor or family room, and one room that served as the playroom for my brother Michael and me. In it we kept a fold-up cot for when my grandmother visited.

Upstairs there were two small bedrooms. They seemed even smaller than they were because of the slanted roof that forced even a little person to kneel in order to peer out the dormer windows. When my grandmother stayed with us, I would rise up early in the morning and scurry down a steep and very narrow staircase into the kitchen and through it turning right into a small foyer that led into the living room. On the right-hand wall of this foyer was a mysterious closet with a short child-sized door. The space was under the stairwell and I was certain a wicked gnome or witch lived in there. To the left was my playroom. On such mornings, I would rush in and creep under the covers next to my grandmother. I don't ever recall that I woke her. She seemed always to be awake for me.

Once I had snuggled up next to her, my grandmother would tell me *Märchen* stories and humorous tales of Armenia and the Middle East. She had fled Turkey with her family after the First World War. Sometimes she would tell me stories of what undoubtedly were her own adventures or of things that she had heard from others as a child, things that *really* had happened. I learned later that when she was a young woman in her teens, she would sneak off to smuggle food and provisions to the Armenian resistance fighters who hid in the hills and countryside. My grandmother told me stories of great big mountain men, "giants," she said, who ambushed people in the passes and catapulted big boulders down cliff sides onto unexpecting travelers. I did not readily distinguish these stories from the fairy tales that she told me. I did not know that some of these stories were also her own worst, haunting memories and nightmares of terrible times.

My life would have been different, maybe even this book would not have been written, had it not been for my grandmother and her stories. She was indeed a captivating storyteller. Now when I am of an age not so far short of what was my grandmother's when she told me her stories, I realize how much my own imagination and sense of humor were formed by her. It is for these stories that I thank my grandmother.

Here in these acknowledgments, I also want to thank my mother and father, Grace and Armen Guroian. They realized that a child whose first language was not English but Armenian needed to be encouraged to read and feel confident about that at a time when there was not much attention paid in our schools to the special needs and the special gifts of bilingual students. Once a week, my father would bring home armfuls of books from the library, and it was my mother's job to answer my every plea for a quick definition of this or that word that I did not know.

What could any of us have become without certain special teachers. This book, which I have written for parents and teachers, is the place to mention two of my special teachers. Helen Rivers was my English teacher and homeroom teacher from seventh through ninth grades. Mrs. Rivers could be a terrifying presence. When she raised her voice she could be heard all the way down into the gym. If you were the object of her outrage or chastisement, you positively shook with fear. Helen Rivers was a taskmaster. I do not know how many poems I had to memorize for her or how many thousands of sentences I diagrammed for her. But when she gave me a big kiss at the ninth grade commencement exercises and left her bright red lipstick on my cheek, I knew I loved her. I realized even then how much she had taught me through the discipline she had cultivated within me with love. Later I also realized that she had given me the essential tools to become a writer.

I attended college at the University of Virginia. And there I had the exceptionally good fortune to have John Graham as a professor of speech and rhetoric. In his courses, he showed me not only the poetics of the English language but impressed upon me the elements of good style. John Graham taught me how to write. And I am immensely grateful to him.

In the Introduction, I mention the late Russell Kirk and his wife Annette and my indebtedness to them both for their encouragement and support in writing this book. But I should also add that Russell helped me procure more than a grant or two that enabled me to take a leave from teaching in order to complete this book. I especially want to thank the Wilbur Foundation for a grant back in 1993 that helped me to begin charting the shape of this book.

Also in the Introduction, I mention St. Paul's School in Brooklandville, Maryland. Both my son Rafi and daughter Victoria attended St. Paul's School. Headmaster Robert Hallett is an inspired educator with a vision. And I am grateful to him for permitting me to bring my research to his school, that is to engage some of his faculty and students in the enterprise of bringing together my college students and their elementary and middle school students to read and talk about fairy tales.

I also want to thank Michael Gorman, Dean of the Ecumenical Institute of Theology at St. Mary's Seminary and University, for recognizing the importance of my work and for arranging several workshops so that I might teach, test my ideas, and learn from teachers and parents. Chapter 1 is based upon the Inaugural Distinguished Lecture in Moral and Religious Education that I gave at St. Mary's Seminary and University under the auspices of the Institute in the fall of 1995. This was published under the title of "Awakening the Moral Imagination: Teaching Virtues Through Fairy Tales" in the Fall 1996 issue of *The Intercollegiate Review.*

Shawn Daley, a brave young undergraduate student at Loyola College, also has earned mention for taking on the otherwise thankless work of making up the index.

Last of all, I am grateful as a father and husband that my children Rafi and Victoria have been in my life. Their joy for life inspired me to read them the stories that are discussed in these pages.

Reisterstown, Maryland V. G.
Epiphany 1998

Introduction

Children are vitally concerned with distinguishing good from evil and truth from falsehood. This need to make moral distinctions is a gift, a grace, that human beings are given at the start of their lives. Of course, we mustn't mistake this grace for innocence. Children are not pure innocents, as every new parent quickly learns. The guile of even the smallest child can make one wonder: "Where did she learn that?" Becoming a responsible human being is a path filled with potholes and visited constantly by temptations. Children need guidance and moral road maps and they benefit immensely with the example of adults who speak truthfully and act from moral strength.

Our society is finding it difficult to meet these needs of children. Some well-meaning educators and parents seem to want to drive the passion for moral clarity out of children rather than use it to the advantage of shaping their character. We want our children to be tolerant, and we sometimes seem to think that a too sure sense of right and wrong only produces fanatics. Perhaps we have become so resigned to flailing about in the culture's muddy waters of moral compromise and ethical obscurantism that it is hard for us to imagine other possibilities for our children. I am no exception. And sometimes I also find myself doing what I often criticize in others, nervously rationalizing my laziness or unwillingness to cultivate conscience and a moral sense in my own children. Mostly we fall back on the excuse that we are respecting our children's freedom by permitting them to determine right from wrong and to choose for themselves clear goals of moral living. But this is the paean of a false freedom that pays misdirected tribute to a deeply flawed notion of individual autonomy. We end up forfeiting our parental authority and failing to be mentors to our children in the moral life. This, I fear, is the actual state of things.

Every parent who has read a fairy tale to a young son or daughter is familiar with what I venture to say is a universal refrain of childhood. "But is he a good person or a bad one?" Or, "Is she a good fairy or an evil fairy?" What greater proof or assurance could we want that God and nature have endowed human beings with a moral constitution that needs to be nurtured and cultivated? Yet our society is embracing an antihuman trinity of pragmatism, subjectivism, and cultural relativism that denies the existence of a moral sense or a moral law.

Fifty years ago, C. S. Lewis, author of the popular Narnia Chronicles, wrote a remarkable little book entitled *The Abolition of Man*. In that book Lewis discussed these forces that starve the moral imagination and replace it with utilitarian rationality. He warned of a philosophy of education and childrearing that undermines confidence in moral certitudes and substitutes the dogma that morality is relative to individual desire and cultural context. Such is the *weltgeist* that captures so many modern people. And yet even as we submit ourselves to this "new morality," we continue to want and expect our children to grow up to be good people according to the surer standards of an "older morality." This "is the tragicomedy of our situation," comments Lewis, that while "we clamour for those very qualities [of character and virtue]" in our children, "we are rendering [them] impossible. . . . In a sort of ghastly simplicity we remove the organ and demand the function. We make men without chests and expect of them virtue."[1]

Perhaps it is not surprising that someone who detected such things in the culture went on to write a series of remarkable children's fantasy stories—the first and best known of these being *The Lion, the Witch and the Wardrobe* —that invite the modern child into a world in which the "old morality" reigns and retains its compelling vigor. Lewis, of course, was heir to the Victorian retrieval of the fairy tale. And he followed in the footsteps of the nineteenth-century inventors of a modern genre of fairy tale and fantasy stories, among whom we must certainly count Hans Christian Andersen and George MacDonald.

The Victorians brought fairy tales into the nursery because they saw in them the capacity to stimulate and instruct the moral imagination. In our day we have witnessed a resurgence of this interest in the fairy tale. The renowned psychiatrist Bruno Bettelheim lent an important impetus to this movement almost twenty-five years ago with his publication of *The Uses of Enchantment: The*

Meaning and Importance of Fairy Tales (1975). "It hardly requires emphasis at this moment in our history," Bettleheim wrote, that children need "a moral education . . . [that teaches] not through abstract ethical concepts but through that which seems tangibly right and therefore meaningful. . . . The child finds this kind of meaning through fairy tales."[2]

More recently, former U.S. Secretary of Education William J. Bennett has edited three highly successful anthologies that include ample samplings of classic fairy tales and modern children's stories.[3] With *The Book of Virtues* (1994), *The Moral Compass* and *A Children's Book of Virtues* (1995), Bennett has tapped into a tremendous desire of parents and teachers for assistance and guidance in choosing stories that have the power to shape the character of children.

As a parent raising small children in the 1980s, I too looked for guidance in choosing stories to read to my son Rafi and my daughter Victoria when they had begun to outgrow the big picture book stage. When my children were between the ages of seven and twelve, I read all of the stories discussed in this book. I then took these readings into the classroom, where over the past decade I have taught courses on children's literature in religion programs on the undergraduate and graduate levels.

It all began with a conversation one evening in the fall of 1983 in the lounge of a hotel in Washington, D.C. I had arranged to meet with the late writer and essayist Russell Kirk and his wife Annette, who were in town for a lecture Russell was to give. Russell Kirk had written on occasion about children's literature and practiced his own talent for telling what he liked to call ghostly tales on his four daughters. That evening I ventured to ask him what children's stories were his favorites. And he was quite obliging. He mentioned to me George MacDonald's *The Princess and the Goblin*, Carlo Collodi's *Pinocchio*, a personal favorite of his, and C. S. Lewis's Narnia Chronicles. And he added other such favorites as John Ruskin's *The King of the Golden River,* Oscar Wilde's "The Selfish Giant," and of course the classic tales of the Grimm brothers and Hans Christian Andersen.

Not all of the stories that Russell Kirk mentioned to me that evening and that I have discovered since have made it into this book. Some others, however, are mentioned and discussed in a short annotated bibliography in the conclusion. But Russell and Annette Kirk gave me and my wife June a start at a time when we were no more knowledgeable about children's literature than I am supposing many readers of this book may be. That is why I have written this book: in order to be of some assistance to parents or teachers who desire to learn, as we did, what books and stories to read with children in the midst of a busy life in which time is limited and making the right choices is important.

As I explored further, I was surprised to discover a scarcity of books that introduce and discuss the moral themes in children's literature in an accessible way for parents and teachers. Oxford University Press itself has published such helpful introductions to the history of children's literature as *Children's Literature: An Illustrated History* and splendid edited collections of fairy tales and children's stories like Iona and Peter Opie's *The Classic Fairy Tales* and *The Oxford Book of Modern Fairy Tales*, edited by Alison Lurie. But books that take care to discuss the content and meaning of these stories in relation to the child's understanding and parents' and teachers' concerns about raising their children to be ethical persons hardly exist.

Literary criticism on modern children's literature is a relatively new field of study that has not yet accumulated a substantial or impressive corpus of interpretation. But most of that which is available is for the experts.[4] Psychologists and educators have done studies, but they mostly address the special concerns of the disciplines and almost always with a markedly secular and social scientific slant. Psychological theories about child development often govern these studies. One might have thought that ethicists could do better. Yet religious and philosophical ethicists have not reflected much on children as moral learners or written much on the virtues as taught and communicated in children's stories. Perhaps this is because, like so many others, ethicists too subscribe to the falsehood that childhood is more about socialization than moral formation. In any case, it is far safer to presume that the moral agent is an adult when discussing morality, and that is how most contemporary ethicists choose to proceed.

Thus, my task in this book is a rather simple one. My primary objective is to serve as a helpful guide through some of the most beloved fairy tales and classic and contemporary fantasy stories written for children. I have tried to be of assistance to parents and teachers who want to explore the moral and religious significance of these stories with their own children or students. By and large I have left definitions of childhood and what actually constitutes children's literature to others. All of the stories that are discussed in this book fall into the categories of the fairy tale and the more modern genre of a children's fantasy story. My experience in the classroom with persons ranging in age from eighteen to eighty proven to me the wisdom in C. S. Lewis's observati about the best test of a children's story. In an essay on writing children's stories, Lewis quips: "I am almost inclined to set it up as a canon that a children's story which is enjoyed only by children is a bad children's story. The good ones last. A waltz which you can like only when you are waltzing is a bad waltz."[5]

I am a theologian by trade and so as might be expected, I have been alert not just to moral themes but also to the great religious questions that have been raised by some of the most popular and honored authors of children's stories. More often than not contemporary writers and critics have avoided these religious themes or discussed them with embarrassment, if not outright antagonism. Thus, I have taken up the challenge to explore seriously some of these religious themes. Several of the chapter headings indicate this concern. Themes of love, immortality, evil, and redemption are at the heart of many of the best children's stories; and these themes ought not to be ignored or minimized. I hope that this book is that much better for its serious attention to the religious aspects of these stories and that both the religious and nonreligious reader will benefit.

As I already have mentioned, this book began with my own children—my son Rafi, who as I write this introduction is preparing to graduate from high school and to attend college in the fall, and my daughter Victoria, who is fifteen years of age. That is to say this book came to be in large measure because, like other parents, I thought it was important to read to my children and to choose the right stories for them. I sought out stories that would enrich their imaginations and perhaps supply them with some memories that would positively influence their character and conduct throughout the course of their lives.

There are indications of success. I believe that both my son and daughter are not only better readers but better persons for that special time we spent each evening before bed reading the fairy tales of the Grimm brothers and George MacDonald or the *Märchen* stories and humorous tales from the Middle East and Armenia that my immigrant grandmother told to me when I was a child. I think that my son's willingness to go to a remote village in Armenia in the summer of 1996 to complete the reconstruction of an ancient church toppled by an earthquake was helped by the fact that I told him my grandmother's stories. In his applications to colleges, I also discovered a short essay that Rafi wrote in answer to a question about which books from his childhood meant the most to him. He responded that C. S. Lewis's Narnia Chronicles were the most memorable because they left him with standards to live by. And in a senior English course, he decided to read all of the Narnia books one more time and to write a final paper on Lewis's use of the elements of the classic epic in his stories.

As for Victoria, there has been a wonderful confluence of our early reading with her pursuit of ballet. She has learned through dance how much the fairy tale genre has influenced music and art. In the spring of 1997, the dance company to which Victoria belonged performed a ballet version of *Alice in Wonderland*—she played the part of the Queen of Hearts.

I think that the great fairy stories naturally lend themselves to dance and dramatic enactment. When Victoria was in the fourth grade, I approached her English teacher with the idea of bringing my undergraduate seminar on children's literature into her classroom. We decided that our common text would be *Pinocchio,* and that we would coordinate our efforts so that late in the spring session my students and I would meet with her fourth graders at St. Paul's School in Brooklandville, Maryland, for conversation, and to share poster drawings that depicted scenes or episodes from the story. We would conclude by breaking up into smaller groups to rehearse dramatic enactments of some of these scenes or episodes and gather together to perform these skits for each other.

I recollect quite vividly the reaction of my college students to this experience as they discussed it at our next meeting. They were struck by how much detail the fourth graders remembered and the surprisingly "sophisticated" lessons that they drew from what they had read. My college students confessed with open embarrassment that the fourth graders had seemed to grasp more than they had. The children seemed to understand much better than they did the nature and source of Pinocchio's temptations and backsliding, and were also much less ready to excuse him for the behavior that got him into so much trouble and caused his father such grief. They did not yet believe as modern college students are apt to do that growing up is a straight line—twelve years of primary and secondary education, four years of college, and with degree in hand one is on the way to becoming a complete and successful human being.

Whereas my college students admitted they sometimes got bored with the repetition in the story, the elementary school children were absorbed with that repetition, for it signaled to them their own immediate experiences of attempting and failing to be good and trying again. But even more important, repetition signaled for them life and struggle and overcoming and getting beyond. It signaled happiness. As G. K. Chesterton observes in his spiritual autobiography, *Orthodoxy*, "It is a mark of the essential morality of fairyland (a thing too commonly overlooked) that happiness, like happiness anywhere else, involves an object and even a challenge; we can only admire scenery if we want to get past it."[6] The repeated attempts and failures of Pinocchio and the challenges he faces over and over to be reunited with the object of his happiness—Geppetto, his father and maker, made immediate sense to the fourth graders and held their attention. My college students began to suspect that maybe they had lost something in growing up—a sense of wonder and a yearning for a taste of the other—that might have been better tended and retained if they had been brought up on more of what we were reading in class. Perhaps the fourth graders they had met were actually nearer than they to the wellsprings of human morality and were better served by reading *Pinocchio* than they had been by taking a required college course in ethics.

Repetition signified one other thing to the fourth graders, the importance of which also dawned on my college students. Chesterton observes that when we grow up we tend to think that repetition is a sign of deadness, "like a piece of clockwork. People feel that if the universe were personal it would vary, if the sun were alive it would dance." To the contrary, "variation in human affairs is generally brought into them, not by life, but death; by the dying down or breaking off of their strength or desire. A man varies his movements because of some slight element of failure or fatigue." Whereas repetition, far from signifying monotony and deadness, may signify delight, desire, and vitality. And this is what it seemed to mean for the children of St. Paul's School who had read *Pinocchio*. "A child kicks his legs rhythmically through excess, not absence, of life. Because children have unbounding vitality, because they are spirit fierce and free, therefore they want things repeated and unchanged. They always say, 'Do it again' " because there is such delight in that thing or activity. "It may be," Chesterton concludes, "that God makes every daisy separately, but has never got tired of making them. It may be that He has the eternal appetite of infancy, for we have sinned and grown old, and our Father is younger than we. The repetition in Nature may not be a mere recurrence; it may be a theatrical *encore*."[7] This idea began to occur to my college students. Perhaps we need more intergenerational learning of the sort my class and I experienced at St. Paul's School. Perhaps fairy tales ought not only to take a bigger place in American childhoods but ought to be read by more college students.

In Chapter 1, I discuss what I believe are some of the serious shortcomings of contemporary education as regards to the moral instruction of our children and the role fairy tales and fantasy stories might play in improving these deficiencies. The views I express have been formed and confirmed by the kinds of experience in the classroom that I have related. The honest self-assessment of my undergraduate students at Loyola College has in no small measure assisted me in writing this book and giving it a purpose.

Yet I also have taught parents and teachers in graduate level courses at the Ecumenical Institute of Theology of St. Mary's Seminary and University in Baltimore, Maryland. And I want to make special note of two workshop seminars that I held at the institute in the summers of 1995 and 1996. These seminars were attended mostly by teachers and pastors, ranging from religious sisters who teach in Roman Catholic parochial schools, to Protestant black ministers of inner-city churches, to lay men and women teaching in public and private schools and Sunday schools. What I have learned from these individuals warrants far more attention than I am able to give here. But much of my inspiration for the contents of this book grew out of these workshops.

In the midst of taking one of my seminars, a black pastor of an inner city church began a series of sermons for adults and children employing some of the fairy tales we were discussing in class. He related these stories to the Bible and social ethical concerns of his ministry. In a striking way, he compared "Beauty and the Beast" with the Old Testament story of Ruth and Naomi. He compared Ruth's love for her mother-in-law Naomi and refusal to abandon her to Beauty's love and loyalty toward her father. And he went on to explain that in her marriage to Boaz, Ruth yet manages to keep her promise never to abandon Naomi. Likewise, even as Beauty keeps her promise to Beast and finally marries him, she reconciles this with her love for and duty toward her father. Another black minister found the resources in "Hansel and Gretel" useful for his work with abandoned and abused children. As he put it: "On any given day we find more than one Hansel or a Gretel on a street corner downtown."

For a final project many of the seminar participants took advantage of the opportunity to write a curriculum outline that they might introduce at their schools and churches. One woman, an elementary school teacher, produced a curriculum outline entitled *A Character Education Unit for Primary Grades.* In it she included a section on moral education and developed a detailed lesson plan using classic fairy tales and modern stories like Margery Williams's *The Velveteen Rabbit.* Three women who are responsible for the education curriculum in local Roman Catholic parishes composed a full-length manual and guide for parents entitled *Learning Virtues and Values Through Fairy Tales for Parent and Child*, designed for a workshop on the sacrament of reconciliation. They wrote sections on child development and story and ritual and provided two extended appendices that introduce selected fairy tales and tools for parents to help them read and discuss these stories with their children.

An Invitation

Thus stimulated by both my readings to my own children and the experience of introducing children's literature in the classroom, I have written this book. I have listened very carefully to the voices of the "nonexperts" (my children and my students) and have tried my best to convey what I have learned from their fresh encounters with the stories discussed in these pages. I have striven to help parents and teachers to find standards in these stories that they might not have seen on their own. But I have wanted also not to spoil the pleasure of reading these stories either for the first or the tenth time. The deep truths of a good story, especially fairy tales, cannot be revealed through discursive analysis—otherwise, why tell the story? Rather, these truths must be experienced through the story itself and savored in the immediacy of the moment that unfolds with the impending danger of the quest or the joy of reunion with the beloved. In George MacDonald's haunting tale, *The Golden Key*, the young heroine of the story encounters the Old Man of the Earth:

> Then the Old Man of the Earth stooped over the floor of the cave, raised a huge stone from it, and left it leaning. It disclosed a great hole that went plumb-down.
>
> "That is the way," he said.
>
> "But there are no stairs."
>
> "You must throw yourself in. There is no other way."

This is also the way it is with fairy tales.

May your own reading of this book be a beginning and not an end, not a closure but an invitation to unceasing explorations of the imagination. And may our children be the ultimate beneficiaries.

1

Awakening the Moral Imagination

When Mendal was already the far-famed and much-hated rabbi of Kotzak, he once returned to the little town in which he was born. There he visited the teacher who taught him his alphabet when he was a child and read five books of Moses with him. But he did not go to see the teacher who had given him further instruction, and at a chance meeting the man asked his former pupil whether he had any cause to be ashamed of his teacher. Mendal replied: "You taught me things that can be refuted, for according to one interpretation they can mean this, according to another, that. But my first teacher taught me true teachings which cannot be refuted, and they have remained with me as such. That is why I owe him special reverence."

Martin Buber, *Tales of the Hasidim*

The American writer Flannery O'Connor spoke a simple but profound truth when she said that "a story is a way to say something that can't be said any other way. . . . You tell a story because a statement would be inadequate."[1] The great fairy tales and fantasy stories capture the meaning of morality through vivid depictions of the struggle between good and evil, where characters must make difficult choices between right and wrong or heroes and villains contest the very fate of imaginary worlds. The great stories avoid didacticism and supply the imagination with important symbolic information about the shape of our world and appropriate responses to its inhabitants. The contemporary moral philosopher Alasdair MacIntyre has summed this up eloquently:

> It is through hearing about wicked stepmothers, lost children, good but misguided kings, wolves that suckle twin boys, youngest sons who receive no inheritance but must make their own way in the world and eldest sons who waste their inheritance . . . that children learn or mislearn what a child and what a parent is, what the cast of characters may be in the drama into which they have been born and what the ways of the world are. Deprive children of stories and you leave them unscripted, anxious stutterers in their actions as in their words.[2]

Musing on the wisdom and ethics of the fairy tale, G. K. Chesterton observes that the genre sparks a special way of seeing that is indispensable to morality. Chesterton writes: "I am concerned with a certain way of looking at life, which was created in me by the fairy tales, but has since been meekly ratified by mere facts."[3] I am calling this way of looking at life the *moral imagination*. Chesterton surely suggests what the moral imagination is when he remarks: "We can say why we take liberty from a man who takes liberties. But we cannot say why an egg can turn into a chicken any more than we can say why a bear could turn into a fairy prince. As *ideas*, the egg and the chicken are further from each other than the bear and the prince; for no egg itself suggests a chicken, whereas some princes do suggest bears."[4] Likewise, we can say that values are set by the free market or by the state and assess what we are up against and how we should trade our wares or parley our talents; but we cannot know, except within the context of the entire story, why what seemed to be courage in one character turned out to be stupid bravado, while what looked like disloyalty in another character turned out to be creative fidelity to a greater good.

THE VIRTUES AND MORAL CHARACTER

Moral living is about being responsive and responsible toward other people. And virtues are those traits of character that enable persons to use their freedom in morally responsible ways. The mere ability, however, to use moral principles to justify one's actions does not make a virtuous person. The late Jewish philosopher Martin Buber tells the story of how he fell into "the fatal mistake of *giving instruction* in ethics" by presenting ethics as formal rules and principles. Buber discovered that very little of this kind of education gets "transformed into character-building substance." In his little gem of moral and educational philosophy, an essay appropriately entitled "The Education of Character," Buber recalls:

> I try to explain to my pupils that envy is despicable, and at once I feel the secret resistance of those who are poorer than their comrades. I try to explain that it is wicked to bully the weak, and at once I see a suppressed smile on the lips of the

> strong. I try to explain that lying destroys life, and something frightful happens: the worst habitual liar of the class produces a brilliant essay on the destructive power of lying.[5]

Mere instruction in morality is not sufficient to nurture the virtues. It might even backfire, especially when the presentation is heavily exhortative and the pupil's will is coerced. Instead, a compelling vision of the goodness of goodness itself needs to be presented in a way that is attractive and stirs the imagination. A good moral education addresses both the cognitive and affective dimensions of human nature. Stories are an irreplaceable medium for this kind of moral education—that is, the education of character.

The Greek word for character literally means an *impression.* Moral character is an impression stamped upon the self. Character is defined by its orientation, consistency, and constancy. Today we often equate freedom with morality and goodness. But this is naive because freedom is transcendent and the precondition of choice itself. Depending upon one's character, an individual will be drawn toward either goodness or wickedness. Moral and immoral behavior is freedom enacted for good or ill.

In the Case of "Beauty and the Beast"

The great fairy tales and children's fantasy stories attractively depict character and virtue. In these stories the virtues glimmer as if in a looking glass, and wickedness and deception are unmasked of their pretensions to goodness and truth. The stories make us face the unvarnished truth about ourselves and compel us to consider what kind of people we want to be.

"Beauty and the Beast" is one of the most beloved of all the fairy tales because it contrasts goodness with badness in a way that is appealing to the imagination. It is also a story that depicts with special force the mystery of virtue itself. Virtue is the "magic" of moral life for it often appears in the most unexpected persons and places and with surprising results. At the beginning of the story, we are told that a very rich merchant had three "daughters [all of whom] were extremely handsome, especially the youngest; [so she was] called 'The little Beauty.' " But nothing more is said about Beauty's physical attributes. Instead, the story draws our attention to her virtuous character. Beauty's moral goodness—her "inner beauty"—is contrasted with her sisters' pride, vanity, and selfishness—their "inner ugliness." Although Beauty's sisters were physically attractive they "had a great deal of pride, because they were rich. They gave themselves ridiculous airs . . . and laughed at their youngest sister [Beauty], because she spent the greatest part of her time in reading good books." By contrast, Beauty was "charming, sweet tempered . . . spoke so kindly to poor people," and truly loved her father.[6]

Because she is virtuous, Beauty is able to "see" the virtues in Beast that lie hidden beneath his monstrous appearance. At her first supper in the monster's castle, Beauty says to Beast: "That is true [that I find you ugly] for I cannot lie; but I believe you are very good-natured." And when Beast tries her even more with his repeated self-deprecatory remarks, Beauty responds emphatically: "Among mankind . . . there are many that deserve [the] name [Beast] more than you, and I prefer you just as you are, to those, who, under a human form, hide a treacherous, corrupt, and ungrateful heart" (p. 190). The sharp contrast between Beauty's goodness and her sisters' badness, which is masked by their physical attractiveness, parallels the irony that the Beast who is repulsive physically is good and virtuous. "Beauty and the Beast" teaches the simple but important lesson that appearances can be deceptive, that what is seen is not always what it appears to be.

Similarly, this great fairy tale also bids us to imagine what the outcome might have been had Beauty's sisters been put in her position. No doubt they would not have recognized or appreciated the goodness beneath Beast's monstrous appearance. Nor does it seem at all likely that they would have made Beauty's courageous and fortuitous choice. The paradoxical truth that the story portrays is that unless virtue is present in a person she will not be able to find, appreciate, or embrace virtue in another.

"Beauty and the Beast" embraces one last important moral truth: a person's decisions in life will define what kind of person she becomes. In this sense also our destinies are not fated: we decide our own destinies. At the end of the story, the "beautiful lady" who has visited Beauty in her dreams appears at Beast's castle and brings with her Beauty's entire family. The fairy then says to Beauty: "Beauty . . . come and receive the reward of your judicious choice; you have preferred virtue before either wit or beauty, and deserve to have a person in whom these qualifications are united; you are going to be a great queen" (p. 195). Beauty's sisters, however, are unhappy in their marriages because they chose their spouses solely on the basis of good looks and wit. Through greed, jealousy, and pride their hearts have become like stone. So they are turned into statues, but retain their consciousness that they might behold their sister's happiness and be moved to admit their own faults.

Awakening the Moral Imagination and Teaching the Virtues

Like all the great fairy tales, "Beauty and the Beast" invites us to draw analogies between its imaginary world and the world in which we live. It supplies the imagination with information that the self also uses to distinguish what is true from what is not. But how, we might ask, is the imagination itself awakened, and how is it made moral? These are important questions for the moral educator, and they are not so easily answered.

Buber's frank discussion of the mistakes he made when he first taught ethics helps us to see how difficult awakening and nurturing the moral imagination is. Buber's mistakes are not uncommon. They are often committed today, especially when the role of reason in human conduct is overestimated and the roles of the will and the imagination are underestimated. This hazard is increased by a utilitarian and instrumentalist ethos that has seeped to the tap roots of our culture. Despite the overwhelming evidence that we are failing to transmit morality effectively to our children, we persist in teaching ethics as if it comes from a "how to" manual for successful living. Moral educators routinely introduce moral principles and even the virtues themselves to students as if they are practical instruments for achieving success. When we tell our children that standards of social utility and material success are the measurements of the value of moral principles and virtues, then it is not likely that our pedagogy is going to transform the minds or convert the hearts of young people. As Buber observed in his own classroom, all that we will accomplish is to confirm the despair of the weak, darken the envy of the poor, justify the greed of the rich, and encourage the aggression of the strong.

Much of what passes for moral education fails to nurture the moral imagination. Yet, only a pedagogy that awakens and enlivens the moral imagination will persuade the child or the student that courage is the ultimate test of good character, that honesty is essential for trust and harmony among persons, and that humility and a magnanimous spirit are goods greater than the prizes won by selfishness, pride, or the unscrupulous exercise of position and power.

The moral imagination is not a *thing*, not even so much a faculty, as the very process by which the self makes metaphors out of images given by experience and then employs these metaphors to find and suppose moral correspondences in experience. The moral imagination is active, for well or ill, strongly or weakly, every moment of our lives, in our sleep as well as when we are awake. But it needs nurture and proper exercise. Otherwise, it will atrophy like a muscle that is not used. The richness or the poverty of the moral imagination depends on the richness or the poverty of experience. When human beings are young and dependent upon parents and others who assume custodial care for them, they are especially open to formation through experiences provided by these persons. When we argue or discuss what kind of education or recreation our children should have, we are acknowledging these realities.

Unfortunately, more often than not, our society is failing to provide children with the kinds of experience that nurture and build the moral imagination. One measure of the impoverishment of the moral imagination in the rising generations is their inability to recognize, make, or use metaphors. My college students do not lack an awareness of morality, although they might be confused or perplexed about its basis or personal ownership. But when they read a novel they are perplexed because they are unable to find the inner connections of character, action, and narrative provided by the author's own figurative imagination. Sadly, the only kind of story many of my undergraduate students seem to be able to follow are news reports and sitcom scripts.

Several years ago, I administered a surprise quiz in a course on theology and literature, in which I asked the students to list and explain five metaphors that they had found in John Updike's early novel *Rabbit, Run*. The majority of the class was unable to name five metaphors. Some students did not even identify the metaphor in the book's title, which I had purposely discussed in the preceding class meeting. It was not that these young people lacked a practical definition of a metaphor. They had been provided with such a definition over and over again in English courses. They lacked, however, a personal knowledge of metaphor that only an active imagination engenders. I suspect that in the past these students had gotten the idea that all they needed to do was look for the so-called facts in a book. Facts are things whose meaning belongs to their use and whose use requires relatively little interpretation. We are living in a culture in which metaphor is discarded for these so-called facts. We train minds to detect these facts much as one breaks in a baseball glove. Meanwhile, the imagination is neglected and is left unguarded and untrained.

WHAT FAIRY TALES DO FOR THE MORAL IMAGINATION

Fairy tales and fantasy stories transport the reader into *other worlds* that are fresh with wonder, surprise, and danger. They challenge the reader to make sense out of those *other worlds*, to navigate his way through them, and to imagine himself in the place of the heroes and heroines who populate those worlds. The safety and assurance of these imaginative adventures is that risks can be taken without having to endure all of the consequences of failure; the joy is in discovering how these risky adventures might eventuate in satisfactory and happy outcomes. Yet the concept of self is also transformed. The images and metaphors in these stories stay with the reader, even after he has returned to the "real" world.

After a child has read Hans Christian Andersen's *The Snow Queen* or C. S. Lewis's *The Lion, the Witch and the Wardrobe*, her moral imagination is bound to have been stimulated and sharpened. These stories offer powerful images of good and evil and show her how to love through the examples of the characters she has come to love and admire. This will spur her imagination to translate these experiences and images into the constitutive elements of self-identity and into metaphors she will use to interpret her own world. She will grow increasingly capable of moving about in that world with moral intent.

When the moral imagination is wakeful, the virtues come to life, filled with personal and existential as well as social significance. The virtues needn't be the dry and lifeless data of moral theories or the ethical version of hygienic rules in health science classes; they can take on a life that attracts and awakens the desire to own them for oneself. We need desperately to adopt forms of moral pedagogy that are faithful to the ancient and true vocation of the teacher—to make persons into mature and whole human beings, able to stand face to face with the truth about themselves and others, while desiring to correct their faults and to emulate goodness and truth wherever it is found. We need to take greater advantage of the power in stories to humanize the young, whether these be Buber's beloved tales of the Hasidim or the stories we commonly refer to as fairy tales.

The Deception of Values in the Contemporary Debate over Education and Morality

"Values" is the chief buzzword of the contemporary educational scene. The word carries with it the full burden of our concerns over the decline of morality. Teaching values, whether family values, democratic values, or religious values, is touted as the remedy for our moral confusion. Of course, this consensus about the need for stronger moral values immediately cracks and advocates retreat when the inevitable question is raised as to which values should be taught. I do not think that the current debate over values lends much promise of clarifying what we believe in or what morality we should be teaching our children. Values certainly are not the answer to moral relativism. Quite the contrary, values talk is entirely amenable to moral relativism.

In *The Demoralization of Society: From Victorian Virtues*

to Modern Values, Gertrude Himmelfarb exposes what some students of Western morals have known for a long time, that "values" is a rather new word in our moral vocabulary. Its use reaches back not much farther than the late-nineteenth century. The German philosopher Friedrich Nietzsche seems to have been the inventor of our modern use of the term as a category of morality. Nietzsche was opposed to what he called "effeminate" Christianity and advocated the "Ubermensch" or superior human being with the courage to defy conventional religious morality and invent his own values. In his famous essay titled *Beyond Good and Evil*, Nietzsche used "values" in this new way, not as a verb meaning to value or esteem something, or as a singular noun, meaning the measure of a thing (the economic value of money, labor, or property), but in the plural form, connoting the moral beliefs and attitudes of a society or of the individual.[7] In his turn of the phrase "transvaluation of values," Nietzsche summed up his thesis about the "death of God" and the birth of his new "noble type of man." Nietzsche described this new kind of human being as "a determiner of [his own] values" who judges right from wrong on the basis of what is good or injurious to himself. Thus, the values of conventional morality were false values bound to be replaced by the self-made values of the truly autonomous and free individual.

Nietzsche's innovative use of the term "values" did not gain immediate approval or acceptance. Even as late as the 1928 edition, the *Oxford English Dictionary* did not list "values" in the plural form referring to moral qualities. More recently, the 1992 edition of the *Oxford Modern English Dictionary* defines "values" not only in the modern sense of moral qualities but assigns them a subjectivistic character. The dictionary's editors give this definition: Values refers to "*one's* standards, *one's judgement* of what is valuable or important in life" (the emphases are mine). Another way of putting it is that "values" belong to those things we call individual lifestyles, and in common discourse a lifestyle is something we choose and even exchange for another according to our personal preferences and tastes, much in the same way that we might replace one wardrobe with another. Himmelfarb is justified when she says: " 'Values' [has] brought with it the assumptions that all moral ideas are subjective and relative, that they are mere customs and conventions, that they have a purely instrumental, utilitarian purpose, and that they are peculiar to specific individuals and societies."[8]

In our consumerist society moral values may even take on the characteristics of material commodities. We easily assume that personal freedom is about *choosing* values for oneself in an unregulated and ever-expanding marketplace of moralities and lifestyles. *Choosing* values turns out to be not much different from shopping for groceries at the supermarket or selecting building supplies at the home improvement store. As a society, we are learning to regard morality and values as matters of taste and personal satisfaction. For some people, married heterosexual monogamy is a value, whereas for others it is romantic relationships with one or several lovers, male or female or both. Some people say abortion is wrong and they do not approve of it; but these same people also say that for others abortion may be all right. This is possible only if values are the creation of the self and are not universally binding moral norms. If one scratches just beneath the surface of the moral outlook of many

Americans, one bumps into the rather naively but also often vehemently held assumption that the individual is the architect of his or her own morality built out of value "blocks" that the individual independently picks and stacks. We suddenly run into the ghost of Friedrich Nietzsche.

There are real and very important differences between what we now call values and the virtues as they had traditionally been understood. Let me put it this way. A value is like a smoke ring. Its shape is initially determined by the smoker, but once it is released there is no telling what shapes it will take. One thing is certain, however. Once a smoke ring has left the smoker's lips it has already begun to evaporate into thin air. Volition and volatility are characteristics of both smoke rings and values. By contrast, a virtue might be compared to a stone whose nature is permanence. We might throw a stone into a pond where it will lie at the bottom with other stones. But if, at some later date, we should want to retrieve that stone from the bottom of the pond, we can be sure that the shape of the stone has not changed and that we will be able to distinguish it from the rest of the stones.

The virtues define the character of a person, his enduring relationship to the world, and what will be his end. Whereas values, according to their common usage, are the instruments or components of moral living that the self chooses for itself and that the self may disregard without necessarily jeopardizing its identity. Accordingly, values are subordinate and relative to the self's own autonomy, which is understood as the self's highest value and essential quality. But when we say in the traditional speech of character that Jack is virtuous and that he is a courageous person, we are saying that the virtue of courage belongs to the very essence of who and what Jack is. Being courageous is not subject to a willing for it to be so or a willing for it not to be so. Virtues and vices define the will itself and also properly describe the willing person. The color orange is both a quality of an orange and an inescapable description of it. If we find an object, however, that looks like an orange but is brown, it must either be an orange that has gone bad or it is not an orange at all. Similarly, it makes no moral sense to say that a courageous man has decided to be a coward. We cannot say on the basis of some subsequent behavior that we have observed in Jack that he must have decided to become a coward. If Jack's late actions were indeed cowardly and not courageous, then we are obliged to revise our original description of Jack.

Thus, I am contending that what seems so self-evident to many of our contemporaries about the centrality of values to moral living might not be true, consistent with human nature, or take into account adequately the larger share of human reality over which we each personally have little or no choice or control. Rather, the best sources in the Western tradition have argued that morality is much more than, indeed qualitatively different from, the sum of the values that an essentially autonomous self chooses for itself. Classical, Jewish, and Christian sources, such as Plato, Aristotle, and Cicero, or Augustine, John Chrysostom, Maimonides, Thomas Aquinas, and John Calvin, insist that morality is neither plural nor subjective. Instead, they maintain that human morality is substantial, universal, and relational in character, founded and rooted in a permanent Good, in a higher moral law, or in the being of God. From this standpoint, values and decisions whose claims of legitimacy extend no further than individual volition are as effervescent as the foam that floats on top of the waves. They cannot be reliable guides to moral living.

The great teachers of our historic culture insist that morality is deeper and more substantial than effervescent foam. It stands to reason, they insist, that where there are waves and foam there is a deeper body of water. These sources describe a sea of substantial morality that lies beneath the ephemeral and ever-changing surface expressions of emotion, taste, and satisfaction in ordinary human intercourse. They describe character as the gravity that keeps us afloat and virtues as the sails that propel us and the instruments that help us to maintain our course, even when the ship is being rocked by stormy waters and high seas.

Sailors need to know when to use ballast or throw down the anchor, lest the ship sink and they drown. In like manner, the virtues enable us to respond correctly to those moments of life that are the moral equivalents to such conditions at sea. However, an ability to discern these moments and respond appropriately entails more than formal techniques of decision-making; just as successful sailing requires that one knows more than precisely the techniques of good navigation. As the latter requires a knowledge of and familiarity with the sea that cannot be taught in books but can only be learned from sea-faring itself, so the moral life requires that we also *be* virtuous. The virtues are not just the moral equivalent of techniques of good sailing; rather, they are the way as well as the end of goodness and happiness. If we assume, however, as so many of the textbooks would have us believe, that problems and quandaries are the whole subject matter of ethics and that the decisions we make are the purpose of morality, then we are likely to interpret even the virtues in the same superficial, utilitarian way that we already think of values. But if we pay heed to the ancient sources, we will recognize that the virtues are related to a much thicker and deeper moral reality. We will see the virtues as the qualities of character that we need in order to steer our way through the complicated and mysterious sea of morality into which we all have been placed. For such journeying a pocketful of values is neither sufficient ballast nor a substitute for sails, compass, or sextant.

Conclusion
On Moral Pedagogy:
A Response to the Contemporary Debate over Moral Education

Years ago in a series of essays entitled, simply enough, "Education, or the Mistake About the Child,"[9] G. K. Chesterton entered into a debate that then was no less important than it is today. That debate is about what counts for moral education. In conclusion, I want to review what Chesterton had to say, thus bringing this conversation around full circle to the claim I made at the start—that stories, especially fairy tales, are invaluable resources for the moral education of children.

Modern educators have not been well disposed toward traditional fairy tales and their like. They write them off as too violent or not contemporary enough and so forth. They favor "practical" and "realistic" stories—stories about the lives children live today that easily lend themselves to distillation into useful themes, principles, and values. What some educators can't find they create. From the pens of textbook writers on values, stories spill whose sole purpose is to clarify so-called moral problems or draw out reasons for making intelligent moral decisions. These stories are of the disposable kind, made to be discarded like empty cartons once the important "stuff" that was packed in them has been removed. Teaching reasoning skills, and not the virtues, is considered the means to a moral education; values-clarification, not character, is regarded as the goal.

These educators think that moral education is like teaching children reading or arithmetic. But that is not even quite accurate, because in the case of moral education children are supposed to be permitted to discover and clarify for themselves their own values and personal moral stance in the world. Yet we do not permit children to invent their own math: we teach them the multiplication tables; nor do we encourage children to make up their own personal alphabets: we teach them how to read. What might be the outcome of an education that did permit children to invent their own alphabets and math? No doubt the result would be confusion or chaos. Should we be surprised at the outcome of our recent efforts to help children clarify their own values, in fact, invent their own personal moralities?

In his own inimitable way, G. K. Chesterton exposed the flaw and deception in this modern approach to moral education. And he identified the dogmatizing in its antidogmatic rhetoric. In our day this modern approach is justified by prior commitments to certain psychological theories that elevate personal autonomy and self-realization above what we dismissively call "external authority." The teacher must not introduce values into the classroom but instead work to "draw out" from children their own moral beliefs and through a process of clarification help them to better formulate their own values. But here is how Chesterton characterized this historic debate:

> The important point here is only that you cannot anyhow get rid of authority in education. . . . The educator drawing out is just as arbitrary and coercive as the instructor pouring in: for he draws out what he chooses. He decides what in the child shall be developed and what shall not be developed. He does not (I suppose) draw out the neglected faculty of forgery. He does not (so far, at least) lead out, with timid steps, a shy talent for torture. The only result of this pompous and precise distinction between the educator and the instructor is that the instructor pokes where he likes, and the educator pulls where he likes.[10]

In answer to the skeptics, Chesterton stated what he thought to be obvious. Whether we admit it or not, education is bound to indoctrinate and bound to coerce. Rabbi Mendal especially thanked and praised his first teacher because he faithfully inculcated in his young student the necessary rudiments of culture and passed on the essentials of a religious and moral way of life. The *Oxford English Dictionary* defines indoctrination as to imbue with learning or bring into a knowledge of something, such as a dogma. Chesterton argued that an authentic moral education is not possible unless something like this occurs. He spoke of the responsibility to affirm "the truth of our human tradition and handing it on with a voice of authority, an unshaken voice. That is the one eternal education; to be sure enough that something is true that you dare to tell it to a child."[11]

The real corruptions of moral education are an imperious moralizing, on the one hand, and the indulgence of spurious argument and undisciplined opinion, on the other. Nevertheless, a valid and effective moral education is bound to be coercive at times and even do a kind of violence, whether or not opinion is "drawn out" from the student or dogma is "put into" him.

> Exactly the same intellectual violence is done to the creature who is poked and pulled. Now we must all accept the responsibility of this intellectual violence. Education is violent because it is creative. It is creative because it is human. It is reckless as playing on the fiddle; as dogmatic as drawing a picture; as brutal as building a house. In short, it is what all human action is; it is an interference with life and growth.[12]

But Chesterton was not an advocate of the blunt and heavy instrument; nor am I. This is one reason why fairy tales appealed to him so much. Fairy tales might not qualify as scientific hypotheses or theories, but they do resonate with the deepest qualities of humanness, freedom, and the moral imagination. At the same time, they deny the psychological and material determinism that lurks behind much of the modern talk of human liberation, and they discredit the hubris of reason and rationality that displaces faith and confidence in truth. Again, they show us a way of envisioning the world—a world in which everything that is need not have been and the *real* moral law connotes freedom and not necessity. The fairy-tale philosopher, wrote Chesterton, "is glad that the leaf is green precisely because it could have been scarlet. . . . He is pleased that snow is white on the strictly reasonable ground that it might have been black. Every colour has in it a bold quality as of choice; the red of garden roses is not only decisive but dramatic, like suddenly spilt blood. He feels that something has been *done*,"[13] that there is something *willful* in all of it, as if someone decided that things ought to be this way instead of another way and that these things are repeated either in order to improve them or simply because they are a source of delight in their repetition. The fairy-tale philosopher respects the deeper mystery of freedom in its transcendent source.

Second, fairy tales show us that there is a difference between what is logically possible and what is morally felicitous, between what is rationally doable and what is morally permissible. In fairy tales the character of real law belongs to neither natural necessity nor rational determinism. Rather, real law is a comprehensible sign of a primal, unfathomable freedom and of a numinous reality and will. Real law, the realest law, can be obeyed or broken, and in either case for the very same reason—because the creature is both subject of and participant in this primal freedom. Fairy-tale heroes are called to be both free and responsible, thus virtuous and respectful of the moral law.

Fairy tales and modern fantasy stories project fantastic other worlds; but they also pay close attention to real moral "laws" of character and virtue. These laws ought not to be high-handedly shoved down the throats of children (or of anyone else). More accurately, they are norms of behavior that obtain in patterns of relation between agent, act, other, and world. Rational cognition is capable of grasping these norms. They become habit, however, only when they are lived, or, as in the case of fairy tales, experienced vicariously and imaginatively through the artful delineation of character and plot in story. Thus, while fairy tales are not a substitute for life experience, they have the great capacity to shape our moral constitution without the shortcomings of either rigidly dogmatic schooling or values-clarification education. By portraying wonderful and frightening worlds in which ugly beasts are transformed into princes and evil persons are turned to stones and good persons back to flesh, fairy tales remind us of moral truths whose ultimate claims to normativity and permanence we would not think of questioning. Love freely given is better than obedience that is coerced. Courage that rescues the innocent is noble, whereas cowardice that betrays others for self-gain or self-preservation is worthy only of disdain. Fairy tales say plainly that virtue and vice are opposites and not just a matter of degree. They show us that the virtues fit into character and complete our world in the same way that goodness naturally fills all things.

I realize that the views I have expressed defy what the advocates of late modernity or postmodernity insist on, that there is no such thing as a common human condition or a perennial literature that lends expression to the experience of that condition. I do not expect to persuade those who are entrenched in these positions to change their minds. I can only appeal to that certain "stuff" of human existence that the human imagination takes hold of and makes moral sense of in fairy tales. I mean such things as: the joy in the birth of a first child and the crippling sorrow of illness and deformity; childhood fears of getting lost matched by childhood desires to escape parental authority; the love that binds siblings together and the rivalry that tears them apart; the naming we do that gives identity and the naming we also do that confuses identity; the curses of dread malefactors and the blessings of welcome benefactors; the agony of unrequited love and the joy of love that is reciprocated.

I could go on. But the skeptics and critics will not be satisfied. The skeptics say there is nothing of commonality in such things, just individual lives and the particular conditions in which these lives flourish or fail. I am not convinced. Nothing of what these people say is proven, and as I grow older and become more traveled and my memory fills with so many different lives and human faces, the wisdom of fairy tales, the wisdom of a common human condition underlying and running through all of the diversity and difference, seems far more reasonable than moral and cultural relativism. One last thing in which I agree with Chesterton. Fairy tales lead us toward a belief in something that if it were not also so veiled in a mystery, common sense alone would affirm: if there is a story, there must surely also be a storyteller.

2

On Becoming a Real Human Child: *Pinocchio*

In the Disney animated film version of Carlo Collodi's classic, Geppetto wishes upon a star that the wooden marionette he has made might become a real boy. In the end, Geppetto's wish is granted by the Blue Fairy because he, Geppetto, has "given such happiness to others" and because Pinocchio has proven himself to be "brave, truthful, and unselfish." The contemporary children's story writer Maurice Sendak judges that Disney's Pinocchio "is good; [and that] his 'badness' is only a matter of inexperience."[1] Sendak likes it this way; as he also dislikes Collodi's *Pinocchio* because the puppet "is *born* bad" into a world that is itself "a ruthless, joyless place, filled with hypocrites, liars, and cheats." According to Sendak, Collodi created a character who is "innately evil, [a] doomed-calamity child of sin" that "doesn't stand a chance . . . a happy-go-lucky ragazzo, but damned nevertheless."[2]

I strongly disagree with Sendak's reading of Collodi. Yet his remarks raise profound questions about the meaning of childhood and about the nature of moral perfection. These matters pertain to Collodi's story and as I will show, contrary to Sendak's opinion, make it one of the great works of literature for children.

What Is Meant by "Growing Up"

Sendak explains that he likes Disney's version of *Pinocchio* because Disney establishes the puppet's desire to grow up as the central concern of the story, rather than emphasizing the imperative to be good. "Pinocchio's wish to be a real boy remains the film's underlying theme, but 'becoming a real boy' now signifies the wish to grow up, not [as in Collodi] the wish to be good."[3] I agree with Sendak that "growing up" is a primary concern in the film, as it is in the book. But his contrast between this desire to grow up and the imperative to be good is troublesome. Surely, Sendak would agree that normally when we say to a child: "It's time you grow up," we mean that in order to become a mature human being, a person must also be morally responsible.

What kind of a story would *Pinocchio* be, after all, if all that was entailed in the fulfillment of Pinocchio's (or Geppetto's) wish is that his wooden frame be magically transformed into human flesh without the accompaniment of an increase in his moral stature? Actually, neither the Disney film nor the Collodi story portrays Pinocchio's wish and transformation into a flesh and blood child this way. In both stories Pinocchio wants to be more, he wants to be a *real* boy, a good boy, a genuine *human* son.

All children, excepting Peter Pan, want to grow up. And, in fact, all healthy children will grow to be adult individuals whether they want to or not. Pinocchio certainly has a special problem that Collodi casts as an allegory about moral growth. Pinocchio is a wooden puppet, and as the blue-haired fairy says to him, puppets never grow: "They are born puppets, they live puppets and die puppets."[4] The deeper meaning belongs to the metaphor of "woodenness." This woodenness of his mind and will and not the matter of being physically made of wood is Pinocchio's greatest obstacle to "growing up." Sendak has this part right at least: Collodi's Pinocchio is no mere innocent, and the wrongs he commits are, more often than not, not merely the mistakes of ignorance, but the consequences of a hard head, undisciplined passions, and a misdirected will that resists good advice.

In the Disney animation, real boyhood is bestowed on Pinocchio as a reward for being good by the Blue Fairy with a touch of her magic wand; or, as the Blue Fairy herself says, because Pinocchio has proven himself "brave, truthful, and unselfish." In Disney's imagination this is magic. In theological terms this is works righteousness. By moral description, the Disney story presents the virtues as the completion and very essence of Pinocchio's humanity—once he has proven himself "brave, truthful, and unselfish" he is transformed into a real boy. Collodi views things differently. In his story, Pinocchio becomes a real flesh-and-blood human child after he awakens from a dream in which the blue-haired fairy forgives him for his former waywardness and present shortcomings, while she also praises him for the good path he has taken by showing a son's love for his father. For Collodi, real boyhood is not so much a reward as it is the visible sign of a moral task that has been conscientiously pursued, a task which even at that moment when Pinocchio is transformed from wood into flesh and blood is not yet wholly completed. Pinocchio's filial love, obedience, truthfulness, and self-expenditure for the sake of others ultimately triumph over his primal propensity to be selfish and self-centered. His good heart with its innate capacity to love finally dominates over his wooden head. The flesh he acquires represents a significant stage in the perfection of his humanity—that is, childhood—when filial love and obedience toward parents are appropriate. These and the other virtues are the preconditions for becoming a real human being, but they do not constitute our humanity as such. Collodi is clear that Pinocchio's good heart is the source and substance of his humanity and that responsible relationships with others are that humanity's path to perfection. Grace assists but does not compel the moral maturation of the puppet, since the puppet, despite Sendak's opinion, is essentially good, and since grace is not the same as Disney's magic.

Tin Soldiers and Marionettes

In *Mere Christianity*, C. S. Lewis asks this hypothetical question:

> Did you ever think, when you were a child, what fun it would be if your toys could come to life? Well suppose you could really have brought them to life. Imagine turning a tin soldier into a real little man. It would involve turning the tin into flesh. And suppose the tin soldier did not like it. He is not interested in flesh; all he sees is that the tin is being spoilt. He thinks you are killing him. He will do

> everything he can to prevent you. He will not be made into a man if he can help it.[5]

In the Disney film, Geppetto wishes that the wooden puppet would become a real boy. In the Collodi fairy tale, Pinocchio makes the wish and not Geppetto; and what Pinocchio actually wishes for is that he become a fully grown man. The blue-haired fairy then explains to Pinocchio that he has to "begin by being a good boy" (p. 132) and that this involves obedience, truthfulness, an education, and consoling one's parents.

Collodi wants his child readers to understand that being a good boy or girl means being in a proper relationship to one's parents. This is the real genius of his story. Pinocchio refers to Geppetto as his father throughout the story. Some of the first trouble he gets into is prompted by his at least half-innocent desire to bring back to his father a fortune that will make Geppetto's life easier. When Pinocchio is separated from his father, his intention is to return. When Pinocchio "loses" his father, his intention is to find him. Over and over, however, Pinocchio is sidetracked by the allurements of quick gain and easy pleasure. He is tested and tried and repeatedly fails to resist temptation. His wooden head, his laziness, selfishness, and rebelliousness, in no small way compounded by his inexperience, overrule his good heart, his innate capacity to love and act responsibly.

C. S. Lewis continues, "What would you have done about the tin soldier I do not know. But what God did about us was this. The Second Person in God, the Son, became human Himself."[6] In this way God not only has called us into the full maturity of being human but he has shown us the way and given us his own strength to see us through. Collodi sends the blue-haired fairy to Pinocchio and at critical moments in the puppet's journey back to his father, she comes to his assistance. Early in the story, she appears as a young maiden who saves Pinocchio from death by hanging on a tree (a clear allusion to the crucifixion of Christ); and she adopts him as her brother. But he is lured away from the fairy child by the wicked fox and cat. Later in the story when Pinocchio returns, he finds that the little house in which the child had lived is no longer there. "Instead there was a little piece of white marble on which these sad words were engraved: HERE LIES THE BLUE-HAIRED CHILD WHO DIED OF SORROW ON BEING DESERTED BY HER LITTLE BROTHER PINOCCHIO." Poor Pinocchio is devastated. He drops to the ground, "kissing the cold stone a thousand times" (pp. 117–18). He counts the fairy child's death as the loss of a sister, now added to the loss of a father. And he blames himself for both deaths.

This is a turning point in the story. The fairy child's mysterious death and the inscription on her gravestone are signs of a grace that does not coerce, but, nevertheless, insists that the wooden puppet become a responsible person. Although Pinocchio lapses again and endures some of the worst consequences of his misbehavior, including being turned into a donkey, something is stirred in his heart, and a memory is lodged there that ultimately contributes to his conversion and transformation into a real human child.

The blue-haired fairy is an immortal who does not abandon Pinocchio. She appears again in the story, for, as Pinocchio discovers, she is yet alive and grown into a young woman. This reunion occurs immediately following an episode in which Pinocchio fails to rescue Geppetto from the sea and has been carried to a place named Busy Bee Island by a friendly dolphin. Pinocchio is desperately hungry but he refuses to work for a meal, until he comes upon a young woman who offers him bread if he will carry a pail home for her. At first, as he accompanies her home, Pinocchio does not recognize who the young woman is. Later, as he has finished eating, he looks up at her with "eyes wide open as if he had been bewitched" (p. 130).

> "What is the matter with you?" asked the good woman laughing
>
> "Because, it's . . . " stammered Pinocchio, "it's . . . it's . . . you are like . . . you remind me of . . . Yes, yes, yes. The same voice . . . the same eyes . . . the same hair . . . You have blue hair too, just as she had! O dear fairy, O dear fairy, tell me, is it you? Is it really you?" (p. 130)

Collodi has recast St. Luke's postresurrection story about the encounter of two of the disciples with the resurrected Christ on the road to Emmaus (Luke 24:13–31). There too, at first, the disciples do not comprehend who it is that is walking with them. But when the resurrected Christ invites them to break bread with him, their eyes are opened. And so it goes in Collodi's story also. This episode of hidden and revealed identity clarifies the providential and nurturant role of the blue-haired fairy. The fairy subsequently asks Pinocchio how he was able to recognize her and he responds, "It was love for you that told me" (p. 131). Having lost a sister, and, as he believes, a father also, Pinocchio asks if he might have a mother. "Now I am a woman, nearly old enough to be your mother," she says. "I like that very much," he says, "because instead of calling you little sister, I shall call you mother." He adds, "a mother, as other *boys* [have]" (my emphasis) (pp. 131–32).

The theme of filial love and responsible relationship with parents and siblings is, as I have stated already, at the very core of Collodi's story. Being a real human child means being a responsible and beloved son or daughter. Being good is not a means to gaining boyhood or girlhood as a reward. Rather, being good is a quality of respect and responsibility toward others you love, firstly and especially one's parents and siblings. This, insists Collodi, is essential to becoming a complete human being. A status as son or daughter, brother or sister, and mother or father deeply defines our humanity.

The Meaning of the "Heart"

In this connection it is also easy to commit another mistake made by Sendak. Sendak is uncomfortable with what he describes as Collodi's excessive emphasis on moral rules. And Collodi certainly does pepper his tale with proverbs and moral precepts that are delivered by such colorful characters as the blue-haired fairy, a cricket who meets an early demise at Pinocchio's hands but returns as a ghostly source of wisdom and conscience, a parrot, and a white blackbird. Yet these proverbs and moral precepts are in service to the much greater ends of love and moral responsibility. Their "externality" is taken into Pinocchio's good heart and they are translated into the "flesh" of his humanity, as the puppet learns to live in the spirit of mature sonship with an inward desire to be good.

Collodi gives us a Christian and catholic interpretation of the "heart." He makes it the seat and source of integral personhood, the innermost self or I. The heart represents all that is potential in us that is wholly human, as we are created in the very image and likeness of God. But the heart, while it is essentially good, is also susceptible to corruption: there good and evil struggle for dominance. In Collodi's story, we follow this struggle through a puppet pilgrim's progress until at last goodness triumphs in the heart, as it should, as is natural; and Pinocchio is moved toward obedience and compassionate care of his father and mother.

In the book's final chapters, Pinocchio not only bravely saves Geppetto from the belly of the great shark, he also turns over a completely new leaf as he devotes all of his energies to provide for his sick father. When he hears that the blue-haired fairy is also very sick in the hospital and without a penny to buy a piece of bread, he even gives over the extra money he has saved to purchase himself a new suit so that his "kind mother" will be cared for (p. 228). The evening of the same day, Pinocchio retires exhausted and dreams that the fairy visits him. She kisses him and says, "Brave Pinocchio! In return for your good heart, I forgive you all your past misdeeds. Children who love their parents, and help them when they are sick and poor, are worthy of praise and love, even if they are not models of obedience and good behaviour. Be good in the future, and you will be happy" (pp. 228–29).

Sendak describes this as "dreary" sermonizing. He calls the fairy's love a "castrating love" and describes Pinocchio's obedience to Geppetto as an unhealthy "yield[ing] up of himself entirely, unquestioningly, to his father."[7] Which moves me to ask: Have we come so far that we readily regard selfless filial love, conscientious respect of parents, and diligent obedience to them as suspect, as the unsavory products of extreme parental severity and abusive dominance over the child?

Pinocchio's Journey: How He Became a Real Human Child

In the end, as the reborn flesh and blood Pinocchio looks at the marionette, his former self, leaning lifeless against a chair, he exclaims: "How ridiculous I was when I was a puppet! And how happy I am to become a real boy!" (p. 232). This is a startling image—a metaphor for life lived to its completion wherein life's complete measure is God's own judgment mirrored in our consciences. In Collodi's story, Pinocchio's humanity is present from the start inside that mysteriously animate piece of wood out of which Geppetto fashions the puppet—a prehistory not told by Disney. The wood is Pinocchio's own recalcitrant nature, that is, a nature affected by a will turned against that nature's own good. The puppet must overcome this destructive willfulness in order to become a faithful son and real human child.

Truthfulness and Self-Narrative

Collodi combines the parable of the prodigal son with the story of Jonah and the whale and Bunyan's *Pilgrim's Progress*. To that mix he adds his own genius. His story verges on merely the episodic—a rogue's tale—but so do our lives if we think about it. It is up to Pinocchio to make more of his life than just a rogue's tale. To do so he must become able to interpret his world and his own purposes truthfully. Collodi employs self-narrative to carry this out. Thus, at critical moments in his adventures, Pinocchio makes attempts to tell his story. These are benchmarks in his moral and spiritual journey of self-discovery, conversion, and transformation. He is able to tell his story more truthfully as time goes on, until at last he narrates the true story of a prodigal son who has found his way back to his father and is forgiven. This is the same story the reader has read.

Equally important, Collodi shows that there is a connection between this truthful self-narration and the ability Pinocchio gradually acquires to interpret reality accurately and to respond to it successfully. Very early in the story, Pinocchio makes his first try at a self-narrative. He endeavors to explain to Geppetto what has happened to him after running away from home. The misadventure reaches its miserable end when Pinocchio returns home tired and cold and burns his feet on the coal heater. Pinocchio's account of the sequence of events is confused. The combination of his inexperience with a propensity to shift blame onto others makes for a rather bizarre narrative. Pinocchio confuses physical or natural causality with moral causality. He exclaims: "I got more and more hungry; and for that reason the little old man with the nightcap opened the window . . . [and] I got a kettle of water on my head" (p. 35).

The innocence or naiveté of a small child might be all that is involved here. But more seems to be suggested than that. "It thundered and lightninged," Pinocchio continues, "and I was very hungry, and the talking cricket said, 'It serves you right; you have been wicked and deserve it.' And I said, 'Be careful cricket!' And he said, 'You are a puppet, and you have a wooden head!' And I threw a hammer at him, and he died; but it was his fault, for I didn't want to kill him" (p. 35). In the second instance, Pinocchio lies, or at least twists the truth, about what the cricket said to him so as to shift blame for the cricket's demise onto the cricket. Even at this early stage of his life, Pinocchio exhibits the rudiments of conscience. Children learn these strategies of excuse-making and transposition of blame onto others early and they can readily identify with Pinocchio. They, like the puppet, also experience themselves as often at the mercy of external forces. The notion that who I am is mostly what is done to me and what happens to me, rings true to a young child's subjective experience. Pinocchio is a puppet. But being a young child is very much like being a marionette.

Having read this story to my own son and daughter and discussed it with fourth grade students, boys and girls, at St. Paul's School in Brooklandville, Maryland, some years ago, I can say the following with surety. First, children especially remember the cricket's admonitions and good advice and how he rebukes Pinocchio for his mendacity and unwillingness to listen. Second, they take a great interest in what comes to pass as Pinocchio turns into a donkey, which the cricket prophesies happens to children who are lazy and disobedient. And last, they are anxious to discuss the nature of Pinocchio's misbehavior and the reasons for his repentance.

In his small gem, *A Brief Reader on the Virtues of the Human Heart*, the philosopher Josef Pieper recalls a popular saying of the Middle Ages: "A man is wise when all things taste to him as they really are."[8] This sums up why people need to look at reality without deceiving themselves. So long as self-deception lies at the source of a person's perception of things, he or she cannot mature into the fullness of being human or lead a successful course through life. In *Pinocchio,* the physiological metaphor of hunger represents the many other passions and desires that lead children astray. Like all small children, Pinocchio is often driven by uncontrollable hunger. This gets him into much of his early trouble; while undisciplined passions and wonderlust eventually land him in the false paradise of Playland. But Pinocchio's longing to be a real boy with a mother and father lies deeper still and is the source of his eventual salvation.

Imagination and the Moral Self

The complete truth about being a human being is often falsified or at least partially obscured by a young child's subjective experience. A person has to grow as a moral self in order to transcend this childlike subjectivity and primitive narcissism. He must begin to take a view of the world that is conditioned by an internal discipline of the passions and a "receptivity to teaching [and] . . . willingness to accept advice."[9] It is certainly what Pinocchio's pilgrimage toward maturity is about. This mature way of experiencing and knowing the world is not the objective knowing normally associated with physical science; nor is it the subjectivity of solipsism. It is an intersubjective and relational way of experiencing and knowing. It is a way of interpreting the world that requires memory and a moral imagination; otherwise a moral self cannot come into being.

Just as the appetites require discipline that they may be directed toward their proper ends, so the imagination needs to be guided by reason, sound memory, and the common stock of human wisdom about the world and its possibilities. Pinocchio's journey to real boyhood and sonship is dependent upon the presence and appropriation of these things that serve his deep desire to be a real boy and human son. As we have seen from his first try at accounting for his behavior and the world around him, Pinocchio initially lacks a robust moral imagination. The rudimentary imagination he has is corrupted by phantasmagoria. Initially, the vain imaginings of Pinocchio's own egocentricity dominate. Freud calls this the "imaginary," thus suggesting a disconnection with reality; earlier philosophical and literary sources merely call it "fancy." But the phantasmagoria of unrestrained appetite and wild passion arise as if willing themselves into existence. The moral imagination is different. The analogies and sentiments of the moral imagination need to be nurtured and cultivated.

In order to abscond with the few gold pieces that were given to Pinocchio by the showman Fire-eater, the fox and the cat persuade the inexperienced puppet that if he buries his gold pieces in the Field of Miracles a money tree will grow that will make him and his father wealthy. Pinocchio's imaginings become wild and fantastic:

> Suppose, instead of a thousand gold pieces, I find two thousand on the branches of the tree? Oh, what a fine gentlemen I shall be then! I shall have a magnificent palace, and a thousand wooden ponies and a thousand stables to play with, a cellar full of lollies, and cordials, and a library brimful of candies, and tarts, and cakes, and almond biscuits, and cream puffs! (p. 98)

These and other phantasmagoria of the untrained imagination lead Pinocchio into many of his misadventures and leave him deaf to voices of good counsel. But Pinocchio eventually outgrows these vain imaginings. As his experiences accumulate—relationships with responsible moral agents, the discomforts of following foolish whims and being driven by blind fear, and the spontaneous acts of his good heart when he rescues his fellow puppet Harlequin from Fire-eater's stove or the mastiff Aldirado from drowning—Pinocchio gains a moral imagination. He begins to associate his experiences in a mutually interpretive manner and to see correspondences between these experiences denoting regularities in the ways persons relate to one another and things interact in the world. He especially embraces the moral obligations and responsibilities that connect him vitally to father, mother, sister, neighbors, and even strangers.

Truthful Story and the Real Self

As I have said, Pinocchio's ability to piece together an accurate account of himself and his adventures increases from beginning to end. The last two accounts are his most successful. Nor do I think it is accidental that they are elicited by events which recapitulate the biblical motifs of drowning and rebirth and penance and baptism into new life.

The first of these occasions follows Pinocchio's misadventure in Playland where he is changed into a donkey. Pinocchio arrives at a circus where again misfortune follows him when he becomes lame in a performance. Of no use now to his owner, the donkey is sold to a man who intends to use his thick skin to make a drum for the village band. The man ties a stone to Pinocchio's neck and throws him into the sea to drown, "so that he might skin him" afterward (p. 199). When the man pulls Pinocchio out he discovers to his amazement and utter dismay that there is a wooden puppet at the end of the line.

> When [the man] recovered he could only stammer, "Where . . . where is the little donkey I threw in the water?" . . .
>
> "I am the little donkey!" answered the puppet, laughing. . . .
>
> "But how can it be that you, who were a little donkey a short while ago, have now become a wooden puppet?"
>
> "It must be due to the sea water. It does, sometimes, work real miracles!" (p. 201)

The spirited puppet then asks the man if he would like to hear "my *true* story" (my emphasis) (p. 201). This is the first time that Pinocchio prefaces his remarks with "my true story." The fall into beastliness is reversed. The puppet who was created in the image of a real boy is returned to his original form. But more seems to have occurred inwardly than even the miraculous transformation of appearance. Pinocchio has become a new person who truthfully tells the story of his adventures. This truth is more, however, than merely a quality of literal accuracy. Truth comes from the heart. And Pinocchio now speaks from the heart:

> "A couple more words, and I'll have finished. After buying me, you brought me here to kill me; and as you pitied me, you preferred to tie a stone to my neck, and throw me into the sea. . . . [But] you reckoned without the fairy."

> "And who is the fairy?"
>
> "She is my mother and, like every mother, she loves her child dearly, and never loses sight of him, and helps him in all his troubles, even when, because of his foolishness and his naughty ways, he deserves no help. So, as I wanted to say, as soon as the good fairy saw I was in danger of drowning she sent an immense shoal of fish who thought that I was a dead donkey, and began to eat me. . . . [And] you must know that when the donkey's hide that covered me from head to foot, was eaten away, naturally the bones remained—or, to be exact, the wood; for as you see, I am made of very hard wood." (p. 203)

Pinocchio acknowledges the great mystery of his transformation in the ocean waters and that nothing less than the providential and motherly love of the blue-haired fairy accounts for it and for his salvation. This confession reflects an inward conversion of heart manifested outwardly by the metamorphosis from a donkey back into a puppet and finally into a real human child.

Love and Courage: Becoming a Real Human Child at Last

Pinocchio manages to escape from the man by diving into the sea and is guided by the blue-haired fairy—who has taken the shape of a she-goat standing atop a rock that juts from the water. As he swims toward the rock, Pinocchio encounters the great shark and is swallowed. Like Jonah in the belly of the whale, he is stricken with fear and desolation. And like Jonah he laments his condition and pleads for salvation. "At first Pinocchio tried to be brave; but when he knew for certain that he was inside the shark's body, as in a prison, he began to weep and sob" (p. 207). But this desperate situation turns out to be the occasion when his father forgives him. For Pinocchio is reunited with Geppetto in the belly of the great shark and when he sees him exclaims: "Yes, yes, it's really me! And you've already forgiven me, haven't you? Oh dear Father how good you are! And to think that instead I . . . oh!"[10] Pinocchio repents and insists on telling his whole story to Geppetto; and it is a truthful telling. In complete command of his memory, he is able to look upon himself without self-deception. The puppet lets go of his old self completely in order to save the life of his father, as he gains the courage, in the face of certain death, to plan a successful escape.

This entire episode inside the shark's body is reminiscent of St. Augustine's thoughts in the *Confessions,* when he speaks penitently of his abandonment of God and self. "But where was I when I looked for you? You were there before me, but I had deserted even my own self. I could not find myself, much less find you."[11] One can hardly doubt in this instance the influence of Collodi's early seminary and theological education.

After Geppetto expresses his complete despair of ever escaping to safety, Pinocchio is able to console his father and give him hope. He already has experienced the horror of death and the redeeming hand of a loving and forgiving providence. He says to his father, "Give it a try, and you'll see. In any case, if it's written in Heaven that we must die, at least we'll have the great consolation of dying clasped together."[12] Josef Pieper writes, "Every brave deed draws sustenance from preparedness for death, as from the deepest root."[13] And Pieper continues:

> To be brave is not the same thing as to have no fear. To be sure, fortitude excludes a certain kind of fearlessness, namely, when it is based on a mistaken appraisal and evaluation of reality. This sort of fearlessness either is blind and deaf toward actual danger or else stems from a reversal in love. For fear and love limit one another: one who does not love does not fear either, and one who loves falsely also fears falsely.[14]

The modern abridgments and retellings of *Pinocchio*, of which Disney's is only the most well known, soften the violence of death in Collodi's original tale and as a result also sweeten and sentimentalize the love that grows within Pinocchio. Thus, they also fail to capture the gritty nature of the puppet's courage and endurance. Pinocchio's close calls with death, whether when dangling over the showman's fire, hanging from a tree, or being plunged into the dark depths of the sea, are also the hard lessons he learns about the true value of life, the reality of reciprocal love, and the necessity of self-expending love in the face of evil and danger.

All of this is beautifully and forcefully captured in the scene that immediately follows the expulsion of father and son from inside the belly of the sea monster.

> While Pinocchio was swimming towards the land as quickly as he could, he noticed that his father, sitting on his back with his legs in the water, was trembling violently, as though feverish.
>
> Was he shivering because of cold, or of fright? Who knows? . . . But Pinocchio thought he was frightened, and tried to comfort him, "Courage,

daddy! In a few minutes, we shall reach land, and be safe."

"But where is the land?" asked the old man. . . . Poor Pinocchio pretended to be cheerful, but was rather discouraged.

He swam until he could breathe no longer: then he turned to his father, and said, "Daddy, help me . . . I am dying!"

Father and Son were about to drown together, when a voice, like a badly tuned guitar, said, "Who is dying?"

"I, and my father!"

"I recognize your voice! You are Pinocchio!"

"Right. And who are you?"

"I am the tunny fish, your pal in the shark's body."

"How did you escape?"

"I did the same as you, but you showed me the way. I followed you, and I, too, escaped."

"Dear tunny, you've come just in time! I beg you, for the love you have for your own children, the little tunnies, to help us, or we are lost."

"Of course! With all my heart."

Reaching land, Pinocchio jumped down first, and then he helped his father. Then he turned to the tunny, and said in a trembling voice, "My dearest friend, you have saved my father's life! I cannot find words to thank you. May I give you a kiss as a token of my eternal gratitude?"

The tunny put his nose out of the water, and Pinocchio, kneeling on the ground, pressed a loving kiss on its mouth. At this sign of real, unaffected love, the tunny, who was not used to such things,

> was so moved that, ashamed to be seen crying like a babe, he dived under the water, and disappeared.
>
> Meanwhile, the sun had risen. (pp. 217–18, 219)

I needn't point out the resurrection symbolism of that last line. Perhaps the profoundest lesson that Carlo Collodi teaches in his magnificent tale is that death too must be faced honestly if love is to become completely real in our lives and in the lives of those who are the recipients of that love. Death *is* the great despoiler of life; but there is the even greater truth that death is powerless over life if love is received and love is returned. I agree with Collodi's deep sentiment here that it is our great human task to learn and believe this truth about life, love, and death; otherwise, how can we possibly grow into better and more perfect human beings. Indeed, if we fail to take this truth to heart, we risk devolving into jackasses or, worse still, wild apes dressed up in men's and women's clothes. As Lucy fears in C. S. Lewis's *Prince Caspian*, "Wouldn't it be dreadful if some day in our own world, at home, men [and women] started going wild inside, like the animals here [in Narnia], so that you'd never know which was which?"[15] Comically, tragically, and, sometimes, ruthlessly, Collodi explores this mystery. In spite of that, his book is not so dark, as Sendak would have us believe. We all must experience some darkness, otherwise how can we appreciate the light? We all must experience the nearness of despair, otherwise, how can we know when to celebrate the triumph of hope? We all must at some time or another face forthrightly the tragedy of love and death, so that one day the pain of separation might be replaced by the joy of reunion with the beloved one.

Pinocchio puts his true courage in the service of a self-emptying love that saves his father's life. He thanks the tunny humbly on his knees for rescuing not *himself* but his *father.* His gratitude is the natural reaction of a loving heart that wholly embraces goodness, represented so movingly in the kiss that Pinocchio presses on the tunny's mouth. And from this moment on, Pinocchio's loving heart is linked with the sequence of all his actions in such a manner that the natural and supernatural virtues of courage, obedience, truthfulness, industry, charity, and compassion surpass his "wooden" propensities for laziness, lying, and selfishness. Already before his wooden frame turns into flesh and blood, Pinocchio is a good son. Thus, not through some final magical action is Pinocchio's transformation into a real boy accomplished, as Disney has it, but by the inner working of a grace that converts the heart and moves the self toward acts of real love.[16]

3

Love and Immortality in *The Velveteen Rabbit* and *The Little Mermaid*

I had at first considered including a discussion of Margery Williams's modern classic *The Velveteen Rabbit* in the preceding chapter. After all, the interest in this wonderful fairy tale is sustained by the Velveteen Rabbit's desire to become real. He gains his first knowledge of what that means from the wise old Skin Horse in the nursery. But we must not overlook the fact that it is the Velveteen Rabbit himself who brings up the question and that *his* desire to become real lies at the heart of Margery Williams's story.

In *Pinocchio,* Collodi emphasizes the need for the puppet to love others and in so doing overcome a deadly self-centeredness. Williams emphasizes the other pole of love's reciprocity—being loved by another. Loving and being loved make us *real*, say these authors, and the stories they have written state that fact powerfully. Yet, in my view, Williams's story explores an even deeper meaning of becoming *real*—immortality. This can be said also of Hans Christian Andersen's universally loved story *The Little Mermaid,* which I will turn to in the second half of this chapter.

I do not think that modern people have outgrown the yearning for immortality, even if it might be the case that the traditional religious answers to the question of immortality are proving less persuasive to many people today than in preceding times. And there is no doubt in my mind that the *The Velveteen Rabbit* and *The Little Mermaid* continue to address the need that children have for satisfying answers to such questions as: "What happens to us after we die? And where do we go?" The renowned psychiatrist Robert Coles, who has devoted a long career to the care and study of children, writes concerning the deep curiosity that his child patients have about immortality. In his book, *The Spiritual Life of Children*, Coles comments:

> The questions Tolstoy asked, and Gauguin in, say, his great Tahiti triptych, completed just before he died ("Where Do We Come From? What Are We? Where Are We Going?"), are eternal questions children ask more intensely, unremittingly, and subtly than we sometimes imagine.[1]

Meanwhile, it is remarkable what lack of serious attention is given to these themes by literary critics and educators, as if religion does not exist in children's lives or, if it does, that it is off limits. It is my contention that Williams and Andersen have written stories that are profound allegories of love and immortality. And I think it is more than worthwhile to explore the messages in these two stories.

On the Meaning of Becoming "Really Real" in *The Velveteen Rabbit*

> One day the Velveteen Rabbit asks the Skin Horse,
>
> "What is REAL? Does it mean having things that buzz inside you and a stick-out handle?"
>
> "Real isn't how you are made," said the Skin Horse. "It's a thing that happens to you. When a child loves you for a long, long time, not just to play with, but REALLY loves you, then you become Real."[2]

The Skin Horse, who has lived in the nursery longer than any other toy, certainly speaks from a wisdom about what becoming real really means. Since his arrival in the nursery as a Christmas gift, the Velveteen Rabbit has wondered whether the mechanical wind up toys are more "real" than he. He assumes this is so since they replicate the movements of real living things and boast of the same to him.

The Skin Horse quickly corrects this misperception. "'Real isn't how you are made,' said the Skin Horse." Indeed, the fate of most of these new mechanical toys is to break and be thrown out. "He [the Skin Horse] knew that they were only toys, and would never turn into anything else." The sources of their very pretensions to being real are ironically also the reasons why they will never "turn into anything else." Their complicated workings leave them easy to break, and they are not soft or lovable like the Velveteen Rabbit. They simply do not possess the traits that will engage the imagination and win the love of a child over a long time. The Skin Horse again puts these matters plainly:

> You become [Real]. It takes a long time. That's why it doesn't often happen to people who break easily, or have sharp edges, or who have to be carefully kept. Generally, by the time you are Real, most of your hair has been loved off, and your eyes drop out and you get loose in the joints and very shabby. But these things don't matter at all, because once you are Real you can't be ugly, except to people who don't understand.

The Skin Horse tells the Velveteen Rabbit that he was made real by the uncle of the boy who now lives in the nursery. He has lost much of his brown coat and the hairs from his tail, but he explains that looking worn out, having failing eyes and weakened limbs, and losing one's hair are the emblems of having been loved and having given oneself in love to another over a lifetime. In time the Velveteen Rabbit, too, becomes old and shabby. The Boy "loved him so hard that he loved all his whiskers off, and the pink lining to his ears turned grey, and his brown spots faded. . . . [But] he didn't mind how he looked to other people, because the nursery magic had made him Real, and when you are Real shabbiness doesn't matter."[3]

This is how in this story the question of what it means to become real is raised. But the answer is not simple. In fact, Williams introduces several levels of meaning. First, the Velveteen Rabbit is quite literally a "real" stuffed animal. This literal meaning of real is taken for granted, however, and is not what the drama and mystery in the story are about. The Velveteen Rabbit wants to become real in quite another sense. He wants to be loved. The Skin Horse testifies that to be loved brings about "realness." In Martin Buber's terms, an "I" embraces another as "Thou" and "realness" comes into being.

This once happened to the Skin Horse, and it also happens to the Velveteen Rabbit. For the Boy eventually tires of the mechanical toys, and embraces the neglected stuffed animal in imaginative play, as if the rabbit were a living being, a person, a "Thou" and not an "It." As Buber said, "Real living is meeting."[4] The Boy's love for the Velveteen Rabbit is analogous to the love shared between two "real" persons in a relationship of mutual affirmation and responsibility. This, in turn, is analogous to the love of God that gives each one of us being and, according to biblical faith, draws us through our own response to his love into immortal life.

Of course, Buber's concept applies to this "real world," in which toys like the Skin Horse and the Velveteen Rabbit are merely inanimate objects and do not possess the powers of thought and speech. And while fairyland and this world hold some things in common, not all things that are possible in fairyland are possible in the "real world." It is not likely that in the "real world" a prince and a pauper could look so alike that through a series of accidents they trade places, but it is possible; whereas, only in fairyland can a wooden hobby horse grow wise or a stuffed rabbit become a creature of real flesh and blood. When a child is drawn imaginatively into fairyland, toys become playmates that are to him every bit as "real" and "alive" and "responsible" for their behavior as himself. Every true nursery or playroom is a piece of fairyland and is a place where metaphors may shade into full-blown allegories of the world outside.

The Meaning of Immortality

Margery Williams surely intended for her story to find its way into the nursery and the playroom where it could stir the child's imagination to make allegory out of metaphor. After the Velveteen Rabbit becomes real like the Skin Horse, one would suppose the story might end. What greater joy in fairyland is there than for a stuffed animal to be made real by the love of a child? Instead, the story takes a turn that strongly suggests, indeed invites, allegorical interpretation. Love lends encouragement to the heart's desire for immortality. Williams believes in that yearning and beckons children—and also willing adults—to freely exercise their imaginations in such a way that the metaphor of becoming real expands into an allegory of immortality.

One day long after the Velveteen Rabbit had become real, the Boy becomes ill with scarlet fever and the doctor orders that everything that has come in contact with him be put into a sack and burned. The Velveteen Rabbit spends the night out in the garden in the sack along with lots of old picture books and all sorts of odd rubbish. As he lays covered in darkness, the Velveteen Rabbit longingly remembers his life with the Boy, the love and the play that they had shared together in this garden, and the happiness that he had known in becoming real.

On one occasion, the Boy had left the Velveteen Rabbit in a cozy spot by the bracken. He was approached by some rabbits who moved like the mechanical toys; yet they were not mechanical at all. Evidently they were "a new kind of rabbit altogether." And they, in turn, quickly discovered that the Velveteen Rabbit had "no hind legs," and that he didn't "smell right" either. They dared him to dance. But, of course, he could not. So he said, "'I don't like dancing,' . . . But all the while he was longing to dance, . . . and he would give anything in the world to be able to jump about like these rabbits." Worst of all one of the rabbits had called out, "He isn't real at all! He isn't real!" The Velveteen Rabbit protested, "I *am* Real!" But he suspected that there was a difference between his realness when with the Boy and being real like these rabbits who ran free and danced in the garden. And he wanted to be like those rabbits.

Williams places this scene midway through the story, but it foreshadows the ending also. As the Velveteen Rabbit lies in a heap in the garden that last night, he thinks sadly, "Of what use was it to be loved and lose one's beauty and become Real if it all ended like this?" His soulful lament is soon anwered in an unexpected way. He does not realize that becoming real in the nursery is itself just a shadow or image of being wholly real like the rabbits he met that day, and that his return to the garden, his true home, ensures he will become one of them.

During the night, the Velveteen Rabbit crawls out of his death sack to seek the comfort of the garden he loved. "A tear, a real tear," writes Williams, "trickled down his little shabby velvet nose and fell to the ground." Where this *real* tear falls a flower grows up unlike any other flower in the garden, and out of the blossom of that flower steps a fairy who with one kiss bestows on the Velveteen Rabbit the gift of life. "'I am the nursery magic Fairy,' she said. 'I take care of all the playthings that the children have loved. When they are old and worn out and the children don't need them any more, then I come and take them away with me and turn them into Real.'" The Velveteen Rabbit asks if he wasn't real already. And she answers, "You were Real to the Boy because he loved you. Now you shall be Real to every one." And so she carries him in flight to where the "real" rabbits are.

I think that the figurative meaning Williams gives to real in the first instance is easily grasped by most readers young and old: when you love someone long and hard enough something new is brought into being through that relationship that deepens and adds meaning to one's life, and an "I-Thou" relationship is established. Such a relationship can even exist between a person and an inanimate object. But what of this final realness, the life that the fairy bestows on the Velveteen Rabbit? Certainly, one easy way out is to subsume the event under the magic that happens in fairyland. The Velveteen Rabbit is simply transformed from an image or replica of a rabbit into a living and breathing rabbit. Such things happen in fairyland.

But many of the college and adult night school students in religion courses with whom I have explored this story have not hesitated to conclude that Williams has written an allegory not only of love but of immortality. Real in the last analysis stands for immortality: the Velveteen Rabbit is an image and replica of a living rabbit just as every human being is an image and likeness of God. These students interpreted the Velveteen Rabbit as an allegory of how we ourselves reach perfection and immortality. One significant stage in our path toward perfection—to become fully human—is when we are loved by others and learn to return the same. The Skin Horse achieves this stage, but for all his wisdom, he does not anticipate the next stage that would make him "really" real. The Velveteen Rabbit, however, finds the path to this fulfillment. This is through no merit of his own but through his own desire to be a Real Rabbit, and by a Greater Love that cares for the toys in the nursery too much to allow them to be just thrown away after they are "used up."

This is how I have come to read *The Velveteen Rabbit.* When the Fairy brings the Velveteen Rabbit to the other rabbits, she says to them, "You must be very kind to him and teach him all he needs to know in Rabbitland, for he is going to live with you for ever and ever." Williams then adds that "she [the fairy] kissed the little rabbit again. . . . [But] he did not know that when the Fairy kissed him that last time she had changed him altogether . . . he was a Real Rabbit at last, at home with the other rabbits."

The Little Mermaid: Hans Christian Andersen's Allegory of Immortality

> *Do fish complain of the sea for being wet? Or if they did, would that fact itself not strongly suggest that they had not always been, or would not always be, purely aquatic creatures?*
>
> A Letter from C. S. Lewis

Recently, Disney Studios gave *The Little Mermaid* their highest compliment when they made it into a full-length animated movie. Nevertheless, as is typical of Disney, the film version betrays the original story while it also adroitly exploits our society's obsessions with physical beauty and romantic love. But the literary critics have faulted Andersen's original tale for somewhat different reasons than the distortions I have alluded to in the Disney retelling.

Roger Sale is one such critic and his opinions about *The Little Mermaid* are typical. Sale not only says that Andersen's story demeans womanhood but he objects to its religious content.[5] In the Little Mermaid, says Sale, Andersen created a female character who is not only naturally inferior to human beings but must suffer senselessly for the likes of "a dense and careless" male character, the prince, whose life the Little Mermaid saves and whose love she unsuccessfully pursues. Andersen tells his reader that merpeople do not possess an immortal soul, Sale continues, yet "he cannot say what this means . . . since the mermaids seem to lack nothing possessed by human beings except legs. . . . To make socially inferior into sexually inferior, and to make sexually inferior into naturally inferior, is bad enough," Sale continues, "but to make naturally inferior into religiously inferior is sheer desperation." Worse still, he concludes, by having her grandmother tell the mermaid that to have an immortal soul she must gain the love of a man, Andersen "reduces 'soul' to a romantic and sexual prize."[6]

Sale objects to putting "explicit religion" into fairy tales because he says it gets authors into the kind of mess that Andersen is in, in this story. I disagree with that conclusion. I do not think that the religious theme weakens Andersen's story, but I more than suspect that religion confounds this interpreter. Perhaps if Sale and other critics like him—for he is not alone in his judgments—were better able to recognize and appreciate the care and artistry with which Andersen employs religious symbolism in his storytelling, they might reconsider their objections to his work. Instead, such critics have poured their energies into psychological and sociological interpretations of Andersen's person and work, so that his religion is almost always interpreted as the rationalization of his own feelings of rejection in personal life, especially in his relations with women, and his failure to gain social acceptability among the upper class.

Jack Zipes's discussion of Andersen in his study *Fairy Tales and the Art of Subversion* is another good example of this social-psychological approach to Andersen and his work. Zipes argues that "Andersen never tired of preaching self-abandonment and self-deprivation in the name of bourgeois laws. The reward was never power over one's life but security in adherence to power." As for the Little Mermaid, Zipes dismisses her religious yearning as denial and rationalization. Stripped of its camouflage, her behavior in pursuing the love of the prince belongs to an ego that has become "dissociated because she is attracted to a class of people [human beings] who will never accept her on her own terms. . . . Thus she must somehow justify her existence to herself through abstinence and self-abnegation."[7]

But what if we were to take Andersen's religion at face value and not as a psychological cover for his personal insecurities about social status and acceptance? Then, I submit, we might interpret *The Little Mermaid* differently, with an appreciation for its allegorical qualities and valuable moral lessons. In this reading the Little Mermaid's virtues of courage, forbearance, and unselfish love would be seen as the admirable attributes of a healthy and strong character.

The Little Mermaid's Longing for Immortality

From the very start of the story, Andersen describes the Little Mermaid as different from her five older sisters. The sisters are the daughters of the Merking, who is a widower. They live with him and his mother at the bottom of the sea in a beautiful palace with walls of white coral. The royal grandmother promises the princesses that on their fifteenth birthdays they may "go up out of the sea"[8] and see the world above. Andersen's authorial voice adds: "None of them (the princesses) were so full of longing as the youngest, and she was the very one that had the longest wait and was so quiet and thoughtful" (p. 80). The Little Mermaid literally longs to see the world above with its land and sea and human cities. But Andersen carefully fills her longings with symbolic import as he expands metaphor into full-blown allegory.

"Outside the palace there was a great garden," writes Andersen. "Over everything down there lay a wonderful blue glow; you would think that, instead of being on the bottom of the sea, you were standing high up in the air with nothing but sky above and below you. In clear calm weather you could see the sun looking like a purple flower with all that light streaming out from its center" (p. 77). Like Williams in *The Velveteen Rabbit*, Andersen uses the paradisical symbolism of the garden as a principal leitmotif for his allegory. He describes a garden suffused with the color blue, which symbolizes mystery and eternity. The sun shines below "like a purple flower with all that light streaming out from its center," evocative of a numinous reality and the Little Mermaid's attraction to it.

Andersen explains that each of the princesses "had her own little plot of the garden, where she could dig and plant whatever she liked." Each gave her bed the shape of something, a whale or a mermaid. The Little Mermaid, however, made "hers quite round and would only have flowers that shone red like the sun." The circle replicates the sun and connotes eternity. Similarly, the Little Mermaid's love of the scentless flowers that she plants in her garden mirrors her deep desire to see the flowers up above and smell their fragrances. "She found her greatest delight in hearing about the world of men up above. . . . What she thought especially wonderful and beautiful was that up on earth the flowers had a sweet scent" (p. 79).

Eventually, we need to make sense of what Andersen might have intended by making merpeople without souls. But I am reminded here of something C. S. Lewis says in *Letters to Malcolm*. Lewis writes: "What the soul cries out for is the resurrection of the senses."[9] Now great harm can be done to the enjoyment of a story when it is treated like a container filled with symbol treats. And I want to avoid that mistake. Yet I also believe that a full appreciation of Andersen's artfulness and intention in making the Little Mermaid what she is with the desires she has, cannot be understood without paying serious attention to the symbolism he puts into this story.

The following passage, once again describing the Little Mermaid's garden and her relationship to it, seems especially significant:

> She was a strange child, quiet and thoughtful, and when the other sisters decorated their gardens with

> the most wonderful things they had got from wrecked ships, she would only have, apart from the rose-red flowers which looked like the sun high up above her, a beautiful marble statue, a handsome boy carved out of clear white stone and come down to the bottom of the sea with the wreck of a ship. She planted by it a rose-red weeping willow which grew magnificently and hung its fresh branches right over the statue down on the blue sand of the ground, where its shadow showed violet and was in constant motion like its branches—its top and its roots seemed always to be playing at kissing one another. (pp. 78–79)

The Little Mermaid deeply yearns for something more in her life than is given by her familiar world. Her curiosity and sense of mystery help her to discover clues of the "otherness" that she seeks long before saving the prince's life or being told by her grandmother that what the prince has that she does not is an immortal soul. When she does lay her eyes on the prince, the Little Mermaid immediately associates him with the statue. He is its living archetype. And the beauty she sees in the prince reflects the glory of the world above to which she is so strongly attracted. The rose-red willow tree alludes to blood and tears and the passion of the cross. This prefigures the Little Mermaid's own suffering, especially her final act of self-sacrificial love, when she chooses death rather than take the prince's life in order to save herself.

In *Orthodoxy*, his masterful work of Christian apologetics, G. K. Chesterton argues the following propositions that I believe bear directly on our consideration of the story of *The Little Mermaid* as an allegory of love and immortality:

> First, . . . some faith in our life is required even to improve it; second, . . . some dissatisfaction with things as they are is necessary even in order to be satisfied; third, . . . to have this necessary content and discontent it is not sufficient to have the obvious equilibrium of the Stoic. For mere resignation has neither the gigantic levity of pleasure nor the superb intolerance of pain.[10]

The Little Mermaid invites great pain and suffering upon herself because she imagines more for her life and is dissatisfied with the limitations of life under the sea. She will not be resigned to the clear implications of her grandmother's explanation of the conditions of her existence and the difficulty, indeed near impossibility, of transcending those conditions.

Her grandmother tells her that in order to gain an immortal soul a man must "fall in love with [you] so deeply that [you] would be more to him than father and mother." She and the man must be wed by a priest with a vow of "faith here and for all eternity; then his soul would overflow into your body, and [you], too, would have [your] share in human fortune. He would give [you] a soul and yet keep his own" (pp. 90–91).

In pursuit of this end, the Little Mermaid makes a deal with the sea-witch. She trades her beautiful voice for legs and willingly takes upon herself the awful burden of having to endure the excruciating pain when she walks, as if she were stepping on "a sharp knife that cuts [her] and makes [her] blood flow" (p. 94).[11] The reader will be warned not to make such deals with the "devil."

And just in case we need to be persuaded of the potentially tragic consequences of doing so, Andersen paints vividly the suffering and grief that the Little Mermaid endures for that mistake. In addition, there is also the ominous condition of her quest for the heart of the prince, because if she fails she will not only forfeit her three hundred mortal years as a mermaid, but will not gain an immortal soul and must die on the first morning after the prince weds another. Nonetheless, Andersen does not permit his reader simply to conclude that taking her sisters' path and being content with remaining a mermaid is the more admirable or desirable choice. His ability to awaken our moral and religious imagination certainly cannot be overlooked. He uses all of his narrative skills to evoke within his readers the same feelings and struggle with those feelings that the Little Mermaid goes through. In spite of her suffering, he makes it difficult for the reader to disapprove of the decisions that she makes, to dismiss her courage as foolishness, or to deny her deepest yearnings and where they might lead her.

Romantic Love and the Desire for Immortality

Sale argues that Andersen reduces gaining "a 'soul' to a romantic and sexual prize."[12] But I don't think that is it at all. Yes, romantic love is part of what moves the Little Mermaid to her decisions and undertakings. But a desire for the beloved and a yearning for an even greater love and communion are mingled in this haunting tale. Andersen leaves us to wonder which the Mermaid wants more, a man or a soul; or whether it is even possible to disentangle her attraction to his beauty from her desire to have a soul and enjoy immortality.

This is not a flaw in the story. Rather, Andersen brilliantly puts the theme of romantic love into the service of his allegory. Peter Kreeft astutely observes that "an image can easily become an idol, and romantic love [can become] an unusually powerful idol because it is such a powerful image." He adds, however, that "romantic love is [also] a powerful image of the love of God because, unlike lust, it does not desire a possessable and consumable thing (like a body)."[13] We are reminded of Dante's attraction to Beatrice in *The Divine Comedy* and, of course, the ancient tale of the love between Psyche and Cupid that has been interpreted through the ages as an allegory of the soul's journey through life and final union after suffering and death with the divine. Kreeft also reminds us that romantic lovers often mistakenly expect that the joy they seek can be found solely in the beloved, whereas wisdom teaches that the beauty that belongs to the beloved is bound to fade and his embrace, which is, after all, merely mortal, must inevitably release. "Because romantic love is only a prophet," Kreeft instructs, "it breaks when it turns into a god."[14]

Andersen's story does not make romantic love into an idol. To the contrary, the story communicates a serious warning about the harm that such an idol can bring upon its worshiper. After she saves the young prince from drowning, the Little Mermaid sets him on a beach where he is found by a young girl. Knowing that he is now safe and that there is nothing more that she, a mermaid, can do for him, she retreats to the sea. Upon her return home the Little Mermaid grows "even more sorrowful than before. Her one comfort was to sit in her little garden and throw one arm round the beautiful marble statue that looked so like the prince." Andersen adds that she "no longer looked after her flowers" (p. 88) and that the garden grew wild and twisted with vines that climbed among the branches of the willow tree and cast darkness over the place. An inordinate erotic attraction to the beloved is bound to lead to unhappiness and ruin. A marble statue is the first object of the Little Mermaid's desire and yearning for something "beyond"; then comes the young prince. But when she embraces the latter as the final object of her love and yearning for happiness and immortality, the path of her life becomes twisted and dangerous. She makes a desperate deal with the witch of the sea that nearly seals her doom.

The Rising of the Sun and What Is Meant by Gaining an Immortal Soul

The Little Mermaid makes choices, and these choices decide her destiny. Others might have made different choices. But she contributes vitally to her final destiny and the person she eventually becomes. Through her attraction to the beauty of the statue and the young prince, the Little Mermaid is drawn toward a wholly other reality. In the end, the life she thinks she has given up and the promise of immortality she thinks she has lost are returned, in spite of her mistakes, because goodness and mercy and unselfish love conquer within her. That is how I would put it, and this way of putting it reveals an allegory.

After the Little Mermaid makes the pact with the sea-witch, a tale unfolds of unrequited love, heart-breaking disappointment, and silent suffering. While the prince holds great affection for the Little Mermaid and lovingly takes her into the protection and comfort of his household, eros is missing in his fondness for her, and she begins to realize that he will never marry her. Her heart slowly breaks as she continues to endure the frustration of not being able to speak and the terrible agony of walking as if on sharpened knives. There comes a time when the prince must go to a nearby kingdom to meet the young princess of that land. The prince is certain that he will not be able to love her, for his obsession is with the face of the young girl that he saw when he first awoke on the beach the morning after his ship sunk. He does not know that he confuses that memory with his memory of the Little Mermaid who he says reminds him of that girl. When his eyes fall on the princess, he recognizes her instead as the young maiden who he thinks saved his life, and a marriage is swiftly arranged.

The prince, who joyfully tells the Little Mermaid of his discovery and decision to marry, does not know that for her a terrible fate is being sealed by his decision to marry. Her life must end at the sunrise after the wedding and her body will dissolve in the foam on the sea into oblivion. Bravely and without complaint, the Little Mermaid accepts her fate. Following the wish of the prince, she participates in the wedding that is held on board a ship, and she dances more brilliantly than ever before. "Sharp knives seemed to cut her delicate feet," writes Andersen, "but she did not feel it, for the pain in her heart cut yet more sharply. . . . She laughed and danced with the thought of death in her heart." Later she stood alone on board ship and "looked for the first red of morning—the first ray of the sun, she knew, would kill her" (pp. 103–4). Andersen joins together the governing symbols in his story in such a manner that the pathos swiftly yields to a profound situational irony, which secures the allegorical meaning.

The symbolism is unmistakably religious. Andersen repeats the images of the rising sun and the red sky. In this manner he alludes strongly to the beginning of his story, when he acquainted the reader with the Little Mermaid's attraction to the sun, the hope it stirred in her heart, and her love of the "rose-red flowers" that shone in her garden like that sun (pp. 78–79). Now at the close of the story the sun appears once more and, instead of a new life, it seems to promise only death. This is what the mermaid and the reader would believe. But just before the arrival of dawn, her sisters emerge from the deep. They inform her that they have struck a deal with the sea-witch. In return for their long tresses, she has arranged for a way that the Little Mermaid can save her own life. They tell their sister:

> She [the sea-witch] has given us a knife—here it is! Can you see how sharp it is? Before the sun rises, you must thrust it into the prince's heart, and as his warm blood splashes to your feet, they will grow into a fishtail and you will be a mermaid again, and then you can come down to us in the water and live for three hundred years before you turn into the dead salt foam of the sea. Hurry! Either he or you must die before the sun rises! (p. 104)

The wisdom of evil is this: that it uses our personal suffering as well as our greatest hopes and fears to tempt us to sin. The sea-witch offers the Little Mermaid the opportunity to wreak a splendid revenge on the prince in a perverse mockery of ritual sacrifice and eucharistic offering. She can take his life and save her own with a knife that is figuratively connected to the piercing pain in her feet that has afflicted her since she journeyed up above. The Little Mermaid's refusal brings to mind the biblical stories of David and Saul and the several opportunities to kill Saul that David relinquishes. In the David and Saul stories, Saul's irrational jealousy and anger move him repeatedly to throw his spear at David. In the last instance, David, who has become a hunted man, is given the chance to see to it that Saul is killed with Saul's own spear as he lies sleeping in an encampment. But David will not permit his lieutenant to carry out the ugly deed. The spear, of course, symbolizes all of the pain, suffering, and injustice that David has endured at Saul's hands whom he loved as a father.[15] The knife that the Little Mermaid is given serves a similar purpose in Andersen's story.

David's decision to spare Saul saves his soul from darkness. Likewise, we can say that the mermaid's decision to spare the prince at the cost of her own life ironically gains her the immortality she believes she has given up. Midway through the story, the Little Mermaid makes her greatest wish, which is a prophecy, as well, of her future conduct and the direction that her life takes henceforth. She says to her grandmother, "I would give all the hundreds of years I have to live to be a human girl for just one day and then to receive my part in the Kingdom of Heaven" (p. 90). This also is, no doubt, just the sort of "religious" writing that Sale finds objectionable.

I cannot answer for the critic's prejudices. I can point out, however, the skill with which Andersen draws out the meaning of the mermaid's final decision to spare the life of the prince. He makes it at once both the culmination of her life and the fulfillment of her religious quest. When the Little Mermaid's sisters beseech her to kill the prince and come back with them, they finish with the plea, "Do you not see the red streak in the sky? In a few minutes the sun will rise, and then you must die!" (p. 104). Andersen does not need to explain the Little Mermaid's feelings. We can easily imagine what they are. It was not easy for her to leave her family the first time. Now she must repeat that decision. But she remains true to her deepest yearnings for the Kingdom of Heaven, even, ironically, by making a decision that she can only believe promises her own death and extinction.

> The little mermaid drew aside the purple hangings of the tent, and she saw the lovely bride sleeping with her head upon the prince's breast, and she bent down and kissed his fair forehead. She looked at the sky where the red of morning was shining more and more brightly; she looked at the sharp knife and gazed once again upon the prince who murmured his bride's name in his dreams. She alone was in his thoughts, and the knife quivered in the mermaid's hand—but she flung it far out into the waves which shone red where it fell and looked as if drops of blood had spurted out of the water. Once more she looked with half-glazed eyes upon the prince, threw herself from the ship down into the sea, and felt her body dissolving into foam. (pp. 104–5)

Sale calls the prince a "dull and careless man." I disagree. The prince certainly does not "see" what we want him to see, but he does not lack affection or sympathy.

As mentioned before, he takes the Little Mermaid in and acts always with kindness toward her. Nor does he lack the important characteristic of gratitude. He is truly grateful for the act of kindness that saved his life, and to the extent that the Little Mermaid reminds him of the face of the girl he thinks saved him, he is moved to compassion. Needless to say, the prince's "blindness" is disappointing, and the romantic in each of us wants to fault him for not loving her as a lover and taking her as a wife. Unwittingly, he causes the Little Mermaid great sorrow. But this is precisely what makes her final decision to spare his life at what she believes will be the cost of her own life such a powerful lesson of love and forgiveness. The Bible's understanding of love echoes throughout—"If you love those who love you what credit is that to you? For even sinners love those who love them" (Luke 6:32). "No one has greater love than this, to lay down one's life for one's friend" (John 15:13).

Perhaps Andersen ought to have ended his story with the passage I cited above: with its symbolism of sacrifice and rebirth, but also leaving sufficient ambiguity and inconclusiveness to keep the adult reader wrestling with its meaning. But much like Dostoevsky in his novels, Andersen felt compelled to spell out the way toward the happy resolution of his irony. And certainly that was not such a bad decision if Andersen had child readers in mind, because they would need more said about the fate of the Little Mermaid.

The mermaid and the reader quickly learn that the sun to which the mermaid has been so drawn throughout will not become, as she fears, the cause of her dissolution into nothingness. For just as the mermaid throws herself into the sea and feels herself dissolving in it, the sun rises out of the sea "and its rays fell gently and warmly on the death-cold sea-foam; and the little mermaid had no feeling of death upon her." She looks up to that sun and is greeted with a vision of "hundreds of lovely transparent forms" (p. 105), and her body is transformed into one like theirs as she ascends into the air to join them.

"'To whom am I coming?' she asked? . . . 'To the daughters of air!' answered the others." The daughters of the air then tell the Little Mermaid that they, like a mermaid "have no eternal soul" and, like her, they depend "upon the power of another" to finally possess one. But by good deeds, they continue, they can gain a soul after three hundred years. "You, poor little mermaid have striven for the same thing as we strive for. You have suffered and endured, and raised yourself into the world of the spirits of the air. And now you, too, through your good deeds can create an immortal soul for yourself in three hundred years" (pp. 105–6).

These passages might cause more than a little consternation in theological quarters. Is Andersen committed to the heresy of works righteousness? Then again he seems to contradict himself because he also says that mermaids and their kind depend upon another to gain an immortal soul. Which is it? Is immortality a gift or the product of one's own good works? But the legitimate theological objections that might be raised here are probably as misleading and beside the point as the claims made by literary critics that the story and its main character are the products of Andersen's personal feelings of social and sexual inferiority. Andersen's stories have gained their own immortality because generations of ordinary readers have not thought these quirks in

Andersen's character or his apparent deviations from theological orthodoxy to be nearly so important as the truths about human nature and human destiny that they explore. Sale and Zipes would dissolve this wisdom in the solvent of their own disbelief and have us ignore these central truths about life and love and death and immortality. But the readers whom they almost begrudge for standing by this story and its endearing character are not likely to be persuaded.

At the ending, Andersen reveals the meaning of the main metaphor that is behind the allegory. He reports that after listening to the daughters of the air, "the little mermaid lifted her bright arms up towards God's sun" (p. 106). In this great and profound fairy tale, Hans Christian Andersen challenges every reader to contemplate his or her fate if love does not endure and personal immortality is just an illusion. Right from the start, the Little Mermaid will not be content with the answer that she is given. "We can live until we are three hundred years old," says the Merking's mother to the Little Mermaid, "but then when our life is finished here, we are only foam upon the water" (p. 90). That is why the Little Mermaid sets her eyes always on the rising sun, even when she fears that it will be her death. And so we should also ask ourselves: Why would we want our children or ourselves to be content with that answer when immortality has been proffered?

4

Friends and Mentors in *The Wind in the Willows*, *Charlotte's Web*, and *Bambi*

Aristotle said it a long time ago: "Without friends no one would choose to live."[1] Friendships bring a goodness and grace into our lives whose value transcends material measure. What value are wealth or possessions, Aristotle challenges us to consider, without companions with whom to share them? And friendships can make us better persons also by prompting us to think of others besides ourselves. "It is more characteristic of a friend to do well by another than to be well done by," Aristotle continues.[2]

Virtue and the moral imagination are practically inconceivable apart from the rich soil of friendship to grow upon. Certainly, childhood would not be childhood without friends: that seems an incontrovertible truth. And so one is bound when writing on children's literature to consider stories whose principal subject is friendship. In this chapter, I consider three of the most beloved stories in the entire corpus of children's literature: *The Wind in the Willows*, *Charlotte's Web*, and *Bambi*.

Each of these stories explores different qualities of friendship; however, *Charlotte's Web and Bambi* move our reflection on the meaning of friendship toward a consideration of that special kind of "friend" who is a mentor.

The Wind in the Willows: On the Nature of Friendship

Of all the classics of children's literature none, in my opinion, captures the meaning of friendship as profoundly and with such utter simplicity and whimsicality as Kenneth Grahame's *The Wind in the Willows. The Wind in the Willows* is about friendship in perhaps its purest form, where no one friend is superior to the other, while each friend stands to benefit from the unique gifts of the other. Such reciprocity is the principal theme of the relations of the four main characters in Grahame's story. Mole, Water Rat, Badger, and Toad are very different in make-up and disposition. Yet this is what lends such richness to their common undertakings and texture to their life together. Complementarity and not uniformity is the spice that adds flavor to good friendships, with special needs and unique gifts mixed and matched to create strong bonds of companionship. Aristotle argues that a friendship may be called perfect not because the friends are perfect, but because the existence of the friendship itself makes possible their moral perfection. The call of friendships to a perfection of one's character is a theme that ought to be introduced to children, and *The Wind in the Willows* is a good place to start.

The Call to Friendship

Mole is the primal "child" of Grahame's story. We watch him mature to claim an equal footing in friendship with

Rat, Badger, and Toad. It is Mole that I turn to mainly. Mole is the first character to whom we are introduced in *The Wind in the Willows.* At the beginning he is mysteriously drawn out of his familiar way of life underground. "The Mole had been working very hard all the morning, spring-cleaning his little home. . . . Something up above was *calling* [my emphasis] him imperiously, and he made for the steep little tunnel which answered in this case to the gravelled carriage-drive owned by animals whose residences are nearer to the sun and air."[3] This is how Mole's rite of passage begins as he enters upon a greater world than he has ever known, one that is filled with new and exciting smells and sounds and sights. More important, Mole joins a community of animal persons that forever will change his life and make him a better and stronger animal.

Grahame thinks of friendship as a calling. By grace and not just chance are we sent forth into the world for fellowship and communion with others. Friendships even sound the call to a higher and transcendent communion with God. Mole and Rat hear this call in the wind in the willows. It is no accident that Mole's growth into full equality with his new friends is marked by an experience of this higher calling. One night he and Ratty set out onto the river to search for their friend Otter's son, Portly, who has been missing for several days. Just before the breaking of dawn, Rat and Mole hear music among the willows, the pipe of Pan, the "Friend and Helper." They follow that music to its source and find little Portly safe under the protection of Pan. While Grahame employs motifs and characters of pagan myth, the theme of spiritual love, which is the highest form of friendship, taps a deep and ancient tradition of spirituality. That tradition successfully relates friendship to agape and that love to the desire for God.

On their mission of charity, the two friends enter together into this spiritual reality of friendship. On the one hand, this higher friendship is an ascetical achievement. Grahame makes a metaphor out of their boating activity. Rat rows while Mole steers accordingly midstream carefully following "a narrow track [of moonlight] that faintly reflected the sky" (p. 118) in search of the lost and helpless child. On the other hand, the friends' journey is a mystical sojourn. Nature provides the essential metaphors, as the two searchers are carried downstream by wind and water. Mole and Rat "glided onwards. . . . Never had they noticed the roses so vivid, the willow-herb so riotous, the meadow-sweet so odorous and pervading . . . and they felt a consciousness that they were nearing the end, whatever it might be, that surely awaited their expedition." Just before dawn, they arrive at a hallowed ground where the nature god resides. "In midmost of the stream, embraced in the weir's shimmering arm-spread, a small island lay anchored, fringed close with willow and silver birch and alder. Reserved, shy, but full of significance, it hid whatever it might hold behind a veil, keeping it till the hour should come, and, with the hour, those who were called and chosen" (p. 122).

Most contemporary interpreters of Grahame's story dismiss this chapter arguing that it neither captures religious experience accurately nor depicts the artistic imagination faithfully. Critics dismiss the entire episode as an unnecessary and disruptive interpolation into the narrative. Yet I am guessing that Grahame deliberately planted this episode right in the middle of *The Wind in the Willows*. It matters little that his own religious beliefs were heterodox or that he disagreed with some of the essential teachings of the Christian faith. Nevertheless, "Pipers at the Gate of Dawn" parallels the Judeo-Christian understanding of the spiritual perfection of friendship. His hero-friends are rewarded with the numinous presence of the nature god.

> Perhaps he [Mole] would never have dared to raise his eyes, but that though the piping was now hushed, the call and the summons seemed still dominant and imperious. . . . Trembling he obeyed, and raised his humble head; and then, in the utter clearness of the imminent dawn, while Nature, flushed with fulness of incredible colour, seemed to hold her breath for the event, he looked in the very eyes of the Friend and Helper . . . saw last of all, nestling between his very hooves, sleeping soundly in utter peace and contentment, the little, round, podgy, childish form of the baby otter. (p. 124)

We see this vision through Mole's eyes, and it is a crucial moment in his maturation. From here on, Mole assumes a much more active and equal role with his friends.

Pan mercifully erases the memory of Mole's and Ratty's encounter with him, "lest the awful remembrance should remain and grow, and overshadow mirth and pleasure" (p. 125). But little otter's continuing presence no doubt reminds the two friends often of the good service to which they once put their friendship. Grahame also emphasizes the manner in which Mole and Rat responded that day to the vision of the demi-god: "Then the two animals, crouching to the earth, bowed their heads and did worship" (p. 124).

Communion and worship are friendship's proper end when it is raised to its highest spiritual level. Whatever else his critics have had to say about this chapter, Grahame got this just right.

Leisure and the Imagination

> *This day was only the first of many similar ones for the emancipated Mole, each of them longer and full of interest as the ripening summer moved onward. He learnt to swim and to row, and entered the joy of running water; and with his ear to the reed-stems he caught, at intervals, something of what the wind went whispering so constantly among them.*
>
> *The Wind in the Willows*

In an age in which people obsessively shift back and forth from work to working at making recreation, we are in jeopardy of forgetting the value of unplanned leisure and spontaneous play. When the child leaves home we believe he leaves play and goes to work. We say that play is for children. But is this really true? There is an ancient wisdom that says, quite to the contrary, that play is the necessary condition for the establishment and health of a truly social world and the role that friendship plays in it. Kenneth Grahame reminds us of that wisdom in *The Wind in the Willows*. When we take time off from work we sometimes say that we are "killing a little time," as if leisure and play are "breaks" from work or "escapes" from responsibility. Grahame, on the other hand, thinks of play and leisure as preconditions of real selfhood and social belonging and as the very best use that we can make of time because this is when friendships are forged.

We rarely see Grahame's coterie of friends working except, one might say, at being good companions. For friendships to prosper leisure and play are necessary. Friendships need the space and time represented by the open country and the river in *The Wind in the Willows.* Friendships thrive in the open air and wind and sun. Their value is missed or misunderstood in a world in which money is mistaken as the measure of nearly everything and utility becomes the sole test of value. Friendships exist for their own sakes. Yet a healthy social world and culture itself are the felicitous outcome of robust friendships.

The world of leisure and play that Rat, Mole, Toad, and Badger inhabit used to be familiar to children. However, we have grown suspicious of this kind of leisure and play, even for children. The opinion spreads that even children's play ought to be organized and properly supervised. It does not occur to us that this might not be true play. We blur the differences between recreation and pure play. But perhaps we are not yet so far from the experience of the Victorians that we cannot still learn from their wisdom about the meaning and nature of childhood and the role of free and imaginative play. Mole is called out of his womblike home to become a friend to others; and he grows into a mole of character precisely because he plays and makes friendships in the doing. Indeed, he seems to be a character destined for friendship. That is what I think makes him so attractive. He gives us the hope that our lives might prosper and be filled in the same way.

In the first chapter of *The Wind in the Willows*, Grahame describes how Mole discovers the river and happens upon Rat.

> He [Mole] thought his happiness was complete when, as he meandered aimlessly along, suddenly he stood by the edge of a full-fed river. Never in his life had he seen a river before. . . . As he gazed, something bright and small seemed to be twinkling in the heart of it. . . . Then, as he looked, it winked at him, and so declared itself to be an eye; and a small face began gradually to grow up around it, like a frame round a picture. (p. 29)

The river is where leisure is taken and enjoyed: as in the Victorian era, the waterways and estuaries of the English landscape were transformed into places of play and recreation. Mole himself is cast in the very image of the river, as "meander[ing] aimlessly" he arrives at its banks. Rat takes Mole boating and teaches him the ways of the river, the life of this leisure, the opportunities and fruits of which are friendship and real happiness. Friendships—unlike, for example, coworker relationships—are not supervised by another party or assigned to a specific task or pursued for profit. Mole and Rat meet accidentally or by destiny, but not according to a plan. He who goes looking for a friend is the least likely of persons to find a friend.

The river symbolizes a world of leisure and play in which friendships are made and enjoyed. Likewise, it also supplies the significant "stuff" of the moral imagination: it is the inspiration of mental images of self and world that the self then can use to relate successfully with others in friendships, common undertakings, and a shared vision of life. Grahame describes Mole's first encounter with the river this way:

> The Mole was bewitched, entranced, fascinated. By the side of the river he trotted as one who trots, when very small, by the side of a man who holds one spell-bound by exciting stories; and when tired at last, he sat on the bank, while the river still chattered on to him, a babbling procession of the best stories in the world, sent from the heart of the earth to be told at last to the insatiable sea. (p. 29)

Soon Mole meets Rat who becomes his principal interpreter of the "stories" that the river tells. Rat is Mole's guide to the world of imaginative play hosted by the river. Mole, for his part, assimilates these experiences to steer his way successfully in the wider world, so that he takes the initiative that sets in motion the triumphant assault upon Toad Hall that drives out the renegade band of unsavory stouts and weasels who have taken possession of it. Toad Hall is not just the elegant home of Mr. Toad; it is the symbol of the friends' social world that Toad foolishly and selfishly puts at risk.

Play is not "killing time" or an "escape" from work; it is an activity that gives life to the moral imagination. If we are deprived of play, the moral imagination is stunted. But play also can be misused, wasted, or become an obsession that subverts the social world. And this is, of course, what is the matter with Toad's behavior as he pursues fancies that feed uncontrolled appetites. Toad's kind of play is entirely set loose from responsibility, and this is why the friends ultimately act severely in order, as the tough-minded but lovingly wise Badger puts it, to "convert" and "reform" Toad. What else are friends for?

With like meaning, Aristotle says of friendship: "It helps the young to keep from error; it aids activities that are failing from weakness; those in the prime of life it stimulates to noble actions—'two going together'—for with friends men are more able to think and to act"[4]

Needfulness and Friendship

As Aristotle also observed, friendships help to satisfy the neediness we have in common as finite creatures and social animals. If we were gods and entirely self-sufficient, we might be able to do without friends. But we are not gods and so we need friends in order to flourish and be happy. Ironically, this neediness, which is sometimes mistakenly thought of as weakness, is the soil in which the mutuality and reciprocity of friendship grows. As I have already suggested, Mole is especially attractive to children precisely because he is so childlike himself and so helpless at the start. As if from a womb, Mole emerges from under the ground into the sun and the fresh air, open to new experiences but still having needs. Instinctively, he seems to know that only friends can answer those needs. And so he sets off into the world.

Indeed, Grahame shows us through Mole's experience how friendships can form us into stronger and more integrated persons. We begin on a lesser plane and through friendships grow into something greater. When Mole first tunnels his way into the light, he is an inexperienced and timid animal. He journeys through woods and meadows and is frightened by unfriendly creatures; yet his natural curiosity and the "call" to friendship spurs him on. Life underground has been comfortable. But above ground, Mole experiences an exhilarating freedom that he has not known before. He is "emancipated," as Grahame puts it. When Mole strikes a friendship with Water Rat and the others, his life takes a new turn.

Children are born needful. We do not condemn the infant's need for her mother's milk or describe the child's efforts to gain parental affection and care as selfishness. We know that these things must necessarily be provided if children are going to grow from young dependent human beings into healthy and responsible adults. Modern psychology confirms that common stock of human wisdom which says that children ought to have friends, and not just any friends, but the best of friends, not perfect friends, for there are no such persons, but friends with real virtues that in combination contribute to the moral growth of all the friends. In *The Wind in the Willows*, Kenneth Grahame gives us a quartet of endearing characters, friends who together show us the value and importance of this truth.

Charlotte's Web: A Friend as Mentor

In the closing pages of E. B. White's memorable children's story, Charlotte endeavors to explain to Wilbur why she responded to his need for a friend and dedicated herself to saving his life through the ingenious ploy of spinning words in her web.

> "You have been my friend. . . . That in itself is a tremendous thing. I wove my webs for you because I liked you. After all, what's a life, anyway? We're born, we live a little while, we die. A spider's life can't help being something of a mess, with all the trapping and catching flies. By helping you, perhaps

I was trying to lift up my life a trifle. Heaven knows anyone's life can stand a little of that."[5]

Even she, whom Wilbur regarded as so wise and so ingenious, was not without real needs. She in her own fashion needed a friend. Nevertheless, Charlotte's and Wilbur's friendship is different from the friendship of Mole, Rat, Badger, and Toad. From the beginning, Charlotte and Wilbur are not equals. Charlotte is wiser and knows more about the ways of the world than Wilbur, and she cares for him with something that resembles maternal love. Fern, the young daughter of the farmer John Arable, opposes her father's intention to mercifully put the runt pig to death; and so she is the first to save Wilbur's life and to care for him like a mother. But Wilbur is moved to Uncle Homer Zuckerman's farm and there, separated from Fern for most of each day, Wilbur needs closer and more constant care and company. Charlotte supplies this and she becomes the object of Wilbur's greatest love.

As a surrogate mother, Charlotte tells Wilbur bedtime stories and sings him lullabies, teaches him manners, tells him to chew his "food thoroughly and eat every bit of it" (p. 64), encourages him when he is down, and builds up his confidence for the day when he must stand on his own four feet without the benefit of her care. But Charlotte, unlike a natural mother, is able to keep a decided distance from Wilbur. This is symbolized by the fact that her web is beyond Wilbur's reach. Thus, something more is suggested about their relationship that needs naming.

Whereas parents do not choose who their children are or children their parents, Charlotte chooses Wilbur as a friend and Wilbur willingly accepts that friendship. That is, Charlotte is a *mentor* to Wilbur and theirs is a *mentoral friendship*. This takes into account the fundamental inequality in their friendship, while it also keeps in view the important characteristic of mutual affection that belongs to all true friendships. Again, Aristotle is our best guide. In his *Nicomachean Ethics,* he discusses relationships of inequality like Charlotte's and Wilbur's and defines these as friendships of a special sort. "But there is another kind of friendship," Aristotle notes, "that which involves an inequality between the parties, e.g. that of father to son and in general of elder to younger" and the like. In such friendships the love that the lesser gives to the greater makes up the difference. In other words, "when the love is in proportion to the merit of the parties, then in a sense arises equality, which is certainly held to be characteristic of friendship."[6] Without wanting to understate Charlotte's true affection for Wilbur, we still are bound to say that Wilbur's love is of greater intensity and is the more all consuming, just in the same way that his need for a friend is the greater. Yet, according to Aristotle, this is as it should be: a proportionality in love appropriate to kind establishes ground for a true friendship.

But what is a mentoral friendship, and how does such a description help us to understand this story and the special ways in which it is able to speak to children? Mentor has a long history and ancient etymology. It comes from the Greek *menos*, which means mind or spirit, and suggests a strong sense of purposefulness and agency. Mentor is the guise and name the goddess Athena assumes as a counselor to Odysseus's son Telemachus in Homer's epic poem *The Odyssey*. Athena is prompted to take this strategy because Odysseus's delay in reaching home has left Telemachus despairing and unsure. She seeks to encourage him, to counsel him, to make him more the wise and better aware of his own inner resources that he will later draw upon in order to defeat his mother's unscrupulous and ambitious suitors, thus guaranteeing a happy return for Odysseus.

The mentor, therefore, is someone who brings the student to self-knowledge and instills confidence in her charge to pursue a successful course in life. The relationship is not unlike a teacher toward a pupil; and, at least as much as in that kind of relationship, the mentoral relationship is characterized by a fundamental inequality. This describes Charlotte's relationship to Wilbur. She is wiser than Wilbur and is able to give him far more than he can offer to her in return, except his love. By her constant counsel and by spinning such words as "some pig," "terrific," and "radiant" into her web, she builds up his self-esteem.

> Ever since the spider had befriended him, he had done his best to live up to his reputation. When Charlotte's web said SOME PIG, Wilbur had tried to look like some pig. When Charlotte's web said TERRIFIC, Wilbur had tried to look terrific. And now that the web said RADIANT, he did everything possible to make himself glow. (p. 114)

Charlotte chooses her role quite intentionally and with a singleness of purpose that would ordinarily contradict the free spirit of friendship. She must find a way to save Wilbur's life while also guiding him through the performance of tasks that will contribute to that end. Nor does her stake in Wilbur's survival include the futurity of parenthood. By the measure of his life expectancy as a pig, her summer's role in his life is but a short span. In this case the special needs of the "lesser" party call out from the mentor just that which he or she possesses that the "lesser" party needs at the present moment. Charlotte says to Wilbur, "By helping you, perhaps I was trying to lift up my life a trifle." And this is no doubt true in some sense. But it does not explain why Charlotte responded in the first place to Wilbur's anguished plea for a friend and someone to save him from death. Charlotte wanted to help Wilbur live and be happy, and she felt within herself that she had the ability to do so. Nothing he might have added would have made a difference in her determination.

So Charlotte gives constant thought to how she will fulfill her promise to save Wilbur's life. "Day after day the spider waited, head-down, for an idea to come to her. . . . Charlotte was naturally patient" (p. 66). And like a wise teacher Charlotte gives her pupil as much as he can absorb and not more. She guides him to the point when he must take possession of himself and make independent decisions.

That process of mentoring comes to a close at the state fair when Charlotte's own life is wholly spent and she is near death. Until this time there has been little that Wilbur could do to reciprocate in kind for what Charlotte has done for him. When he realizes, however, that Charlotte will not return to the farm and that there is nothing he can do about that, Wilbur takes an initiative that bridges the significant gap between mentor and pupil, sufficient to the requirements of true friendship. Wilbur sees to it that Charlotte's egg sac is gotten back to the Zuckerman's farm where it will be safe. Yet even this act of loving reciprocity is conditioned and limited by the enduring qualities of the mentoral relationship itself. It cannot change Wilbur's relationship to Charlotte from "lesser" to "greater." Wilbur cannot teach the teacher; nor is he able to share in Charlotte's experience of being his guide. The mentor stands at both ends of the "mentor-mentee" relationship, the "mentee" only at one end. Wilbur waits through the long winter until the spring to enter into a role toward Charlotte's children that is similar to what she was toward him. Yet Charlotte's special role of mentor and friend to Wilbur is irreplaceable and unrepeatable. At the end of the story we are told:

> Wilbur never forgot Charlotte. Although he loved her children and grandchildren dearly, none of the new spiders quite took her place in his heart. (p. 184)

If we are able to look back on our lives and say that there was a Charlotte in it, we are most fortunate; but an even greater good fortune is if we become a mentor and friend to someone else, as Charlotte A. Cavatica was for Wilbur the runt pig.

Bambi: What Mentors Are For

Walt Disney so radically altered Felix Salten's *Bambi: A Life in the Woods* that it is difficult not to worry that the reader will keep wanting to return to the Disney animation rather than follow the lines of the original story. Yet Salten's book is one of the most beautifully written of children's stories. It is a tale spun with great poetic force and majesty. As with the two previously discussed books, I have chosen to look closely at one particular character. Here it is Bambi in his relationship with the mysterious old stag. Through this relationship, Bambi grows into full maturity and assumes a special role in the woods. In Salten's tale, this is the central relationship and not Bambi's love for Faline, the young doe, as Disney portrays it.

Thus far, I have led the reader from a discussion of pure friendship in *The Wind in the Willows* through the mentoral friendship in *Charlotte's Web.* In *Bambi,* Salten explores the meaning of pure mentorship. Whereas friendships necessarily entail equality of one sort or another, mentorship presupposes a fundamental inequality between mentor and pupil. The mentor's selection of the pupil is the defining act in such a relationship, since the mentor has a vital stake in choosing the right pupil.[7] He wants to ensure that the special knowledge and skills that he possesses are transmitted to another. Contemporary institutionalized forms of education bend to an egalitarian impulse that inhibits the teacher from discriminating among students. Even the renewed contemporary interest in mentorship as an aspect of professional education is strongly affected by this egalitarian prejudice, so that it is almost assumed that the pupil initiates the relationship with a mentor of his choice. While this might be a legitimate and worthwhile practice in modern education, I do not think it is pure mentorship: the mentor must be free to decide whether or not to take on a pupil or protégé.

Salten has depicted the real thing. The pure mentoral relationship is hierarchical and selective, and is always asymmetrical. The mentor selects or accepts a pupil according to a judgment as to whether the knowledge and special skills he or she owns can be safely or effectively reposed in that pupil. In the mentoral relationship we are nearer to the role of master to apprentice than teacher to student in the modern egalitarian sense.

In contrast to the spirit of modern educational theory, in the mentor/mentee relationship there lies no distinction between method and content. By means of physical gesture, tone of voice, and behavior, the mentor communicates his special knowledge and skill and also a piece of his own character. There is no such thing in this relationship as being informative without also being formative. What kind of friendship is this, if it is friendship at all? I believe that the mentoral relationships that belong to both White's and Salten's stories ultimately indicate friendship. In both stories a relationship of unequals increases affection, trust, and mutuality—all essential earmarks of friendship. But unlike *Charlotte's Web*, in *Bambi* the private lives of the central characters are not the primary concern, and so in the latter story the qualities of friendship that develop within the mentoral relationship are subordinate to and serve the purposes of mentorship. A mentor gives himself over to producing in another essential qualities of character that are not merely private or personal but ultimately crucial to the continuance of a special art or a way of life. In this manner, Salten illumines a form of relationship the conspicuous lack of which in modern society may also help to account for the crisis of morality and culture that we are facing.

The Solitary Life and Life in the Woods

Early in *Bambi* the reader learns that the old stag is the spiritual head and protector of the deer herd, even though he is absent and removed most of the time from their daily lives. Salten echoes the biblical theme of a calling to "separateness." He also incorporates characteristics of both the Stoic sage and the Christian office of the holy elder of monastic origins. The stag is referred to as the old Prince by the other deer of the woods. He is a solitary guardian who appears suddenly, usually, as we learn, when the deer and other smaller creatures need to be warned of danger, especially of the hunter. He is the ideal embodiment of the virtues and practical skills necessary for deer to prosper. The stag is vigilant and he has studied and put to memory the physical topography of the woods so as to be able to avoid or escape immediate danger. "He uses trails none of the others ever use. He knows the very depths of the forest. And he does not know such a thing as danger."[8] He also knows the spiritual geography of life and death in the woods. He practices the virtues of attentiveness and watchfulness that extend and deepen life and living for all of the deer.

The stag commands profound respect and even awe from the other deer. "There isn't anybody that compares to him. Nobody knows how old he is. Nobody can find out where he lives. Very few have seen him, even once. At times he was thought to be dead because he hadn't been seen for so long. Then someone would see him again for a second and so they knew he was still alive. Nobody had ever dared ask him where he had been" (p. 57). The other deer do not mistake him for a god as they do Man; but he is admired as the model of what is highest and noblest in the deer.

The secret of the stag's wisdom and longevity resides in his ability to be "alone," to spend time with himself achieving self-mastery and perfecting his special powers of discernment and insight into the rhythm of the life of the woods. He has perfected a special sixth sense of knowing or anticipating when that rhythm is going to be interrupted by the hunters and the death that they rain upon its inhabitants. Why the stag chooses Bambi as his protégé and successor is not explained. That choice is wrapped up in the mysterious character of the stag himself. What does unfold in the story is a special form of relationship whose process and completion not only defines mentor and protégé but also serves all the deer, since it prepares a new guardian and protector.

The Importance of Knowing How to Be Alone

Salten introduces the theme of knowing how to be alone early in the story. And throughout he explores its importance for survival in the woods. In one sense being alone is what any young buck or doe must learn in the maturing process. It is associated with personal autonomy and gaining the courage and confidence to live apart from the mother in order that mating takes places and the species is perpetuated. Salten is a careful observer of the life and behavior of deer. But he is not just the naturalist recording deer life. He is also a moralist and he uses this natural basis of his story to tell a moral tale. For the moral imagination, "being alone" assumes ethical and spiritual significance.

Early in the story the stag suddenly confronts Bambi. Bambi has been lost and wandering through the woods and thickets. He is frightened and calling for his mother. "What are you crying about?" the stag says to Bambi. "Your mother has no time for you now. . . . Can't you stay by yourself? Shame on you!" (p. 55). This timely reproach sows a seed of desire in the youngster. He wants to be like the old stag and wants to prove himself better in his eyes. For a long time the stag is absent. Bambi struggles on his own to be mature and act independently without fear. He learns some hard lessons about life in the woods, especially about the reality of death. He witnesses the hard and bloody deaths of some of his other animal companions who are killed by natural predators. But he also discovers another presence—human beings kill with an unpredictability and wantonness that terrifies all of the woodland creatures.

On one occasion a young adult buck is shot. Salten carefully describes Bambi's reaction:

> He [Bambi] felt himself threatened by something dark. He did not understand how the others could be so carefree and happy while life was so difficult and dangerous. The desire seized him to go deeper into the woods. They lured him into their depths. He wanted to find some hiding place where, shielded on all sides by impenetrable thickets, he could never be seen. (pp. 68–69)

Salten's story shades into allegory. Man, the hunter, symbolizes the irrationality of evil that always threatens to rob life of meaning. Bambi must understand the nature of the destructive force. In the face of danger and even death he must learn a discipline of vigilance and self-possession. Bambi's desire to go deep into the woods is not a mere impulse to escape. He is driven to be truly free and not be a captive to the blinding and incapacitating fear that he has observed in the other deer and inhabitants of the woods.

At the end of the story, Bambi has learned how to be alone and we are left to understand that the old stag's role and responsibility for the lives of the deer and other animals in the woods now devolves upon him as the stag himself goes off to die. Salten writes: "When he [Bambi] was still a child the old stag had taught him that you must live alone. Then and afterwards the old stag had revealed much wisdom and many secrets to him. But of all his teachings this had been the most important: you must live alone. If you wanted to preserve yourself, if you understood existence, if you wanted to attain wisdom, you had to live alone" (pp. 175-76).

Such a practiced "aloneness" paradoxically is not the homelessness or the desolation that the other creatures experience in the face of danger or evil. Of all the animals and deer, the old stag is the most at home in the woods and the least afflicted by desolation. This is because he understands the order of existence and trusts in its Source. The aloneness to which Bambi is called is a way of learning important skills of survival. In this manner Bambi is made ready to become the guardian of the herd, not that he rules by might, but rather that he leads like the biblical prophet, through discernment and familiarity with the way of Being itself. The old stag brings up Bambi in this singleness of life for the good of all. And the last and most important lesson he teaches Bambi is about the true order of Being. At the close of the story, the old stag leads Bambi to the still and bloodied body of a poacher:

> "Do you see, Bambi," the old stage went on, do you see how He's lying there dead, like one of us? Listen, Bambi. He isn't all powerful as they say. Everything that lives and grows doesn't come from Him. He isn't above us. He's just the same as we are.

He has the same fears, the same needs, and suffers in the same way. He can be killed like us, and then he lies helpless on the ground like all the rest of us, as you see him now."

There was silence.

"Do you understand me, Bambi?" asked the old stag.

"I think so," Bambi said in a whisper.

"Then speak," the old stag commanded.

Bambi was inspired, and said trembling, "There is Another who is over us all, over us and over Him."

"Now I can go," said the old stag. (p. 187–88)

This is the final and most important truth that the old stag teaches to Bambi. With this truth Bambi takes the stag's place as the new guardian of the herd. His new status has been built upon the sure foundation of his obedient relationship to the old stag.

The Special Qualities of the Mentor

In this magnificent story, Salten depicts a special form of love and relationship that the English word "friendship" does not quite cover; and yet mentorship and friendship are related. Before the old stag leaves Bambi to go off and die, he says to him: "Good-bye, my son, I loved you dearly" (p. 188). Never before did the old stag state his love in such words; yet in all of his actions toward Bambi he manifested this love. The mentor is a special "friend." What makes the friendship special is that the stag reserves it in his heart until his role as mentor is completed.

There is a poignant moment in the novel that never ceases to draw attention from students in my classes.

About midway in the story, Bambi happens upon the old stag grazing on grass in a clearing. He decides to go up to the stag and tell him who he is. As he approaches the stag, Bambi feels the stag's strength. The stag returns Bambi a haughty look that really misrepresents his own feelings inside. Bambi is discouraged by what he takes to be the stag's indifference toward him. But the stag is thinking to himself, "What should I say to him? I'm not used to talking. I'd say something stupid and make myself ridiculous" (p. 120). So he decides to walk off, leaving Bambi "filled with bitterness" (p. 121). On the one hand, we could interpret this interlude as a missed opportunity for an intimate friendship to be initiated. No doubt Bambi is greatly disappointed; the stag might have handled things differently. On the other hand, can't we say that, however awkwardly he handled things, the stag did the right thing by not striking up the conversation?

I think the latter is worth considering. This episode is a reminder that the old stag is only a deer and not a god. We recognize that even he needs companionship. And yet had he indulged this need, his role as mentor might have been compromised. Even the old stag is still learning and maturing in the role of mentor; and he is giving something up in order for that role to meet success. In this way, Salten emphasizes how special and difficult this calling is to be a mentor: this is especially true in an age in which emotions are given free reign and friendships come easy and end just as easily. So many modern people experience abandonment and desolation, are afraid to be alone, and will do anything not to be alone. Perhaps this is one reason why true mentoral relationships are missing in modern life.

Can it be we have become too soft or weak and afraid to be true mentors, and are losing the capacity to make and keep lasting friends? The mentor has to be tough and withhold the full expression of "friendship" in order that wisdom and patrimony are passed on. Effective parenthood, as well, may require elements of the mentoral relationship. Children need parents who are good mentors; but they also need mentors who are not parents, who like Charlotte and the old stag are able to keep a studied distance from their young charges. In either instance, these special cases of "friendship" are essential both for the maturation of the individual and for the health and growth of community and culture.

5

Evil and Redemption in *The Snow Queen* and *The Lion, the Witch and the Wardrobe*

A person's goodness or badness is a valence and measure of one's humanity or inhumanity. Because this is true we do not hesitate to call individuals like Adolph Hitler and Ted Bundy monsters, and persons like Mohandas Gandhi and Mother Teresa saints. For sure, in the moral realm most things are not wholly black or wholly white. In most of us goodness and badness are complicatedly mixed. That is why most of us deserve neither the condemnation of monster nor the appellation of saint. But there is no mistaking the whiteness of white for the blackness of black. And if that sounds childlike, so be it.

Even in this jaded age a grown up comes along every now and then who, like a child, affirms this truth without apologies. The late Charles Malik, former president of Lebanon, was one such childlike grown up. Malik said:

> There is truth, and there is falsehood. There is good, and there is evil. There is happiness, and there

is misery. There is that which ennobles, and there is that which demeans. There is that which puts you in harmony with yourself, with others, with the universe, and with God, and there is that which alienates you from yourself, and from the world, and from God. These things are different and separate and totally distinguishable from one another.

I take these sentiments of Malik to be the product not of naiveté and untested idealism but of moral character tried in the human struggle for justice and peace. Malik lends expression to a deep knowing that evil is real and loose in the world and that redemption from the hurt and violence of evil is part our doing and part the grace of God. This struggle is what life is finally all about. Or in the words of the eldest brother Dmitri of Fyodor Dostoevsky's great novel *The Brothers Karamazov*: "The devil is fighting with God and the battlefield is the human heart."

The Redemptive Truth of the Heart

"Man is broad, even too broad, I would narrow him," adds Dmitri. Dmitri is moved to say such a thing by the intensity of his own personal suffering. Ironically, however, this is the expression of a man whose heart is so complex and nature so broad that he could not possibly be other than who he is. The irony is indicated by the very title of the chapter in which this speech is located—"Confessions of an Ardent Heart." The heart represents the center of personal existence, the unifying power of the self, the center of willing and purposive action.

Hans Christian Andersen and C. S. Lewis respected the "broadness" of human nature and believed that if the heart is pure, then goodness will prevail. But if our heart is impure, then more than likely you or I will rationalize and justify our own selfishness and misdeeds. It is not surprising, therefore, that both wrote profound allegories about the struggle between good and evil that is waged within the human heart. Through their stories, these two writers explore how the heart becomes dark and hardened when it follows evil, as well as how redemption from this "fall" is possible through the power of active goodness and love.

The Snow Queen: Whence Evil and How Love?

Now the heart speaks readily and warmly where it is at home. The coldness of the outer spaces chills it into silence.

Austin Farrer, *Love Almighty and Ills Unlimited*

On one level, Hans Christian Andersen's *The Snow Queen* is a romantic's response to the eighteenth-century Enlightenment's emphasis on abstract and utilitarian reason. It is also a satire aimed at a philosophy of education that sharpens the intellect while starving the emotions. *The Snow Queen* transcends romanticism, however, and reclaims a vision of the integral self in communion with others and with the whole of creation. In *The Snow Queen*, Andersen shows us wherein evil lies and how it robs life of joy, but he also celebrates how goodness and love restore wholeness and happiness to life.

The story is in seven parts and is about two young children, a boy and a girl, who live in apartments right next to each other. They are the best of friends, until one day the boy is stolen away by the mysterious Snow Queen.

The Origin and Nature of Evil

Andersen begins his novella-length fairy tale with a prologue. A good frame can illumine and enhance even the best of paintings, and Andersen's prologue accomplishes the same for his story.

It does so by telling this tale: Once upon a time the Devil invented a magic mirror that had a strange power. It made anything that was good or beautiful that was reflected in it look horrid; while everything that was wicked and ugly appeared desirable and attractive. The Devil was the headmaster of a school for demons and his pupils soon broadcast the news that "for the very first time . . . you could see what the world and mankind really looked like."[1] In the end, they decided to fly with the mirror to heaven in order to ridicule the angels and God himself. But as they flew higher and higher, the mirror laughed so hard that the demons lost their grip of the object. And so it fell all the way to earth where it shattered into millions and billions of pieces, some that were so small that the wind blew them to every corner of the world.

This was the worst thing that could have possibly happened because every piece and sliver of the mirror possessed precisely the same power to distort beauty and goodness as the whole mirror. Whenever pieces "got into people's eyes, there they stayed, and then the people saw everything distortedly, or else they had eyes only for what was bad in things. . . . Some people even got a little bit of the mirror in their hearts, and then it was really dreadful, for their hearts became just like lumps of ice" (p. 229).

Anderson's prologue is reminiscent of the story of the

tower of Babel. In that biblical myth human beings, who speak a single language, try to build a tower that reaches to the heavens in order "to make a name" for themselves and rival God (Gen.11:1–9 RSV). God sees that they are grasping beyond their creaturely limits and so he resorts to confusing their speech, thus forcing them to abandon their Promethean project. But, of course, as the Book of Genesis testifies, human beings remain proud and rebellious and pursue other means to gain godlike superiority and control over their fellows.

Andersen's myth of the demons and the broken mirror illuminates the brokenness and discordancy of human existence. Thus while resembling the story of the tower of Babel, it draws also from the biblical story of the Fall and the legend of the proud angel Lucifer's rebellion against God (e.g., Isa. 14:12–15, Zech. 3:1–2). These biblical tales teach that pride, inordinate desire, and egoism interrupt and shatter the harmony and communion of innocent life.

The biblical themes in the prologue thus frame and interpenetrate the story Andersen tells of the love shared between the young girl named Gerda and the little boy Kay, and the strange events that test that love. He begins with a description of a garden paradise, in which the two children play.

> In the big city, where there are so many houses and people that there is not room enough for everyone to have a little garden, and where, therefore, most people must content themselves with flowers in pots, there were two poor children, who had a garden that was a little bigger than a flower-pot. They were not brother and sister, but were just as fond of

> one another as if they had been. Their parents lived right next to each other; they lived in two attics; where the roofs of the two neighbouring houses met and the gutter ran along under the eaves, the two little windows faced one another, one from each house. All you need do was step over the gutter and you could get from one window to the other.
>
> Their parents had a large wooden box outside each window, and in it grew vegetables for their use and a little rose-tree. . . . Then their parents found that if they placed the boxes across the gutter they reached almost from one window to the other, and looked for all the world like two banks of flowers. As the boxes were very high and the children knew they must not clamber upon them, they often got leave to climb out to one another and sit on their little stools under the rose-trees where they played wonderful games together. (p. 231)

So in the beginning, the boy and girl are an indivisible couple. They hold each other's hands and kiss the roses and look "up towards God's bright sunshine" and speak "to it as though the Christ Child were there Himself" (p. 233). They are like Adam and Eve in the garden of Eden before the Fall, when the first couple walked with God and were in unbroken communion with each other and with creation.

One afternoon, however, as Kay and Gerda are gazing with wonder and appreciation at a picture book of animals and flowers, Kay is suddenly stricken. A splinter of the Devil's mirror pierces his heart and another enters his eyes. Immediately, he sees and responds to things differently. He tells Gerda she looks ugly when tears well in her eyes as she fears for him in his cry of pain. He looks up at a beautiful rose and sees a grotesque worm-eaten flower. All of the roses begin to look ugly. And as the summer shades into fall and winter, Kay's heart turns into a lump of ice.

Andersen portrays what traditional religion calls diabolical possession. It is the inverse of love and communion. The self is imprisoned within its own egoism. It is inordinately attracted in an all-consuming manner to some *thing* or *object*. As a result, it is drawn away from the presence of others. Instead, there is only "the burdensome presence of one obsessed by himself, a self-idol."[2]

This is what happens to Kay as he gradually grows mean-spirited and separates himself from Gerda and the world they have shared in perfect communion. Some who think that Andersen is best understood from the vantage of Jungian or Freudian psychology or one or another theory of child development have argued that Kay's behavior after the splinters enter his eye and heart are "normal" signs of male aggressive behavior and of a healthy ego seeking autonomy after the dependency of early childhood. Andersen writes that Kay became bored with his old picture books and said they are for babies. He takes to standing behind the grandmother's chair when she reads, cruelly imitating her characteristic gestures. And "his games had become quite different . . . from what they had been before, they were so intelligent" (pp. 234–35). One recent psychological interpreter contends that all of this is simply evidence that Kay is nearing adolescence.[3]

It is worth noting, however, that illustrators of the story have portrayed the children as pre-adolescent. The tone of the story from beginning to end would justify this artistic judgment. In any case, Andersen the allegorist was not content with literal meanings. Even if he accurately reflects patterns of child development in this story, he transforms these into symbols that probe the deeper meaning of good and evil. His personal faith may have fallen short of the contemporary standards of Christian orthodoxy, but Andersen believed fervently in a liberal version of Christianity that emphasized Jesus' life as a moral model and his teachings of the kingdom of God as an ethic to live by.[4]

Near the end of *The Snow Queen,* Andersen cites a biblical verse to which he was profoundly attracted. It is taken from the gospel of Mark (Mk. 10:15) and becomes the spiritual centerpiece of the story. *"Whosoever shall not receive the Kingdom of God as a little child shall not enter therein"* (p. 262). If we pay heed to this saying, we can not miss Andersen's deeper moral message. He would not have us tolerate Kay's meanness toward Gerda or the grandmother. Kay is being transformed into a little beast, and Andersen is portraying the genesis of this evil. God is the source of goodness and unity. That is why it is so devastating when Kay begins to turn against Gerda and the grandmother. For they not only represent goodness, they are also near to its divine source.

The Appearance of the Snow Queen

The grandmother mentions the Snow Queen to the two children on one stormy day in winter when Gerda and Kay ask her if the snowflakes that swarm in the winter wind have a queen like the bees. She then tells them the story of the Snow Queen, the biggest of all the snowflakes, who never lies down to rest like the others. Instead, she visits the homes of humans and spreads ice flowers on the windows wherever she goes. Gerda is afraid that the Snow Queen might come to visit their home. But Kay boasts, "Just let her try! . . . I should put her on the warm stove and then she would melt" (p. 232).

That night Kay thinks he sees the Snow Queen outside of his window.

> She was very beautiful and dainty, but she was of ice, dazzling, gleaming ice, all through, and yet she was alive; her eyes shone like two clear stars, but there was no rest nor quiet in them. She nodded towards the window and beckoned with her hand. The little boy was terrified and jumped down from the chair; and then it was just as if a great bird flew past the window outside. (p. 232)

This is the stuff of nightmares and subconscious fears and desires. The worst actually happens, however, when one winter day Kay is dragged out of town in his toboggan by the Snow Queen on her great sledge, and so is physically removed from those who truly love him. Andersen then comments: "He [Kay] was completely terrified and wanted to say the Lord's Prayer, but all he could remember were his multiplication-tables" (p. 236). Thus, Kay is disarmed and unable to resist the spell of the Snow Queen. He is the prisoner of his own young ego and inordinate self-love that is symbolized ultmately by his self-imprisonment in her ice castle.

Kay's "captivity" in the Snow Queen's ice castle is not so much a physical incarceration as a spiritual self-subjugation. Kay wants to stay because his heart is frozen by the kiss of the Snow Queen and because she has made him forget Gerda and his grandmother. His heart frozen, all that Kay is left with is his reason, of which he has grown overly proud. The evil enchantress takes advantage of this pride. She promises Kay that if he can just spell one particular word—the word "eternity"—out of the thousands of pieces of ice that lay in a vast frozen lake in the middle of her palace, Kay will become his "own master" and she will "present him with the whole world—and a new pair of skates" (p. 268). Locked up behind the icy walls of the Snow Queen's castle, Kay spends his days "dragging sharp pieces of ice about, arranging them in all sorts of ways. . . . In his own eyes the patterns were quite remarkable and of the utmost importance—that was what the grain of glass that was stuck in his eye did for him!" He lays out his patterns trying to form words. But he was never quite able to "hit upon the way to lay out the one word he wanted, the word eternity" (pp. 267–68). In trying to be the complete master of his own destiny and of the world, Kay is moved by the same kind of hubris that sent the demons up into the heavens with the magic mirror to ridicule God and the angels. This is Kay's personal hell.

Andersen wants us to think of Kay as "everyman" (or "everyboy"). And everyman or everyboy is susceptible to the lure of evil. The twentieth-century Russian religious philosopher Nicholas Berdyaev has written that "the struggle against the Creator is waged not only by those who distort with evil the image of the created world, but also by those who suffer from the evil in it."[5] In *The Snow Queen*, Kay is as much if not more a sufferer of evil as a protagonist of evil. Andersen does not rationalize about this or attempt to sort out the difference. Instead, he lets the allegory speak directly with all of its symbolical force. He reports the "facts" of Kay's predicament in rich evocative imagery. The frozen lake that is broken into thousands of pieces all looking the same is an image (or reflection) of the Devil's shattered mirror. But it might also be interpreted as a metaphor for our hardened and shattered humanity of which each one of us is a broken piece.

Andersen does not propose a theodicy that resolves the big problem about why there is evil and suffering. Nor does he address the more particular questions that his story is bound to raise, such as: "Why did a splinter of the Devil's mirror enter Kay's eye and heart and not someone more deserving of such a fate?" Instead, Andersen turns his attention to how our separated and splintered lives might be made whole again and brought into harmony with one another. As God sent his only begotten Son to rescue humanity, Gerda is sent to rescue Kay. Isn't this how evil is answered and remedied in the course of real living—by love on a mission to reclaim the beloved and restore complete communion?

Gerda's Quest and the Redemptive Power of Love

Gerda searches for Kay all over the world and at every turn resists temptors and temptations that would make her forget Kay and abandon her search. When Gerda finally finds the Snow Queen's palace and readies to enter it, she remembers the Lord's Prayer that Kay forgot; and the breath of her speech forms "itself into bright little angels that grew bigger and bigger as they touched the ground. They all had helmets on their heads and spears and shields in their hands . . . [and] there was a whole legion of them round her" (pp. 265–66). Under this protection, Gerda enters the castle and finds her way to Kay. When she sees him she cries warm tears and recites a hymn of praise that the two of them used to sing in their parents' garden.

> "In the valley grew roses wild.
> And there we spoke with the Holy Child!" (269)

Gerda's words and tears penetrate Kay's heart and thaw it, and Kay himself weeps so bitterly that the grain of glass washes out of his eye. Andersen seems to have believed that the good memories of childhood possess profound redemptive power and are capable of opening our hearts to goodness and love for the rest of our lives. I do not think this is mere sentimentality. A similar thought was expressed by Dostoevsky in *The Brothers Karamazov*. In the closing scene, which I have recalled many times when raising my own children, Alyosha Karamazov, the youngest brother, addresses a group of boys for whom he has become a mentor and role model. This speech is made following the funeral of one of their young comrades whom the boys had once taunted and persecuted but later were reconciled with and came to love. He says:

> You must know that there is nothing higher, or stronger, or sounder, or more useful afterwards in life, than some good memory, especially a memory from childhood, from the parental home. You hear a lot said about your education, yet some such beautiful, sacred memory, preserved from childhood, is perhaps the best education. If a man stores

> up such memories to take into life, then he is saved for his whole life. And even if only one good memory remains with us in our hearts, that alone may serve one day for our salvation . . . and keep [us] from great evil.

A Message for Our Times

We began our discussion of *The Snow Queen* with some comparisons to the biblical story of the Creation and the Fall. I am going to conclude with another comparison to the biblical myth. Like that myth, Andersen's tale illumines one of the most fundamental forms of division and alienation in human experience—the alienation of man and woman from one another. In the Bible's terms, the two whom God intended to be in intimate communion became divided into two opposing sexes. The complementarity of gender was corrupted, the communion was replaced by brokenness and separation, love by lust, and henceforth the sexes play out a deadly and demeaning game of lure and pursuit.

Most of the stories with which our children become acquainted through the popular culture reinforce these distorted and corrupted images of male and female and their relations. The new Generation X sitcoms, which millions of subteen children also watch, humorously objectivize the body as a specimen for sexual browsing and fantasy. Sexual love is depicted as a sport in which the game includes rules made up as you go along. This is the rotten fruit of a decadent romantic love. The culture's already depraved vision of the romantic lover is now being transmuted into the image of the sexual user. Baseness, selfishness, and even ruthlessness are often presented humorously so as to seem like desirable traits of character.

The Snow Queen answers this twisted message of the contemporary stories of our lives that are scripted by the new myth-makers of prime time television. Near the end of her journey, Gerda finds the home of a Finnish woman—an archetypal wise woman who possesses great magical powers. She sees what is at stake in the success or failure of Gerda's quest: Kay's humanity and Gerda's own completeness. As she tells the reindeer, whom she enlists to lead Gerda to the palace of the Snow Queen, "They [the splinters] must be got out [of his eye and heart] first, otherwise *he'll never be human again"* (my emphasis) (p. 264). The reindeer pleads with her to give Gerda "'the power to put everything right." But the old woman answers with perhaps the most significant statement of any character in the story: "I can't give her greater power than she has already!" She declares: "Can't you see how great that is? Can't you see how she makes man and beast serve her, and how well she's made her way in the world on her own bare feet? She mustn't know of her power from us—it comes from her heart" (p. 264).

In a book on *The Snow Queen* with which I find myself mostly at odds (because of its psychological analysis), Wolfgang Lederer, however, hooks the reader to a very important point. He asks, "What if Kay were not rescued, were not redeemed by Gerda? He [would] continue his frigid intellectual games amid the vacuous light show of the aurora borealis forever—and he would never *come alive.*" Lederer claims that Gerda, taking the initiative, brings Kay alive again by restoring between them the communion of love. "The most moving passages of the story," Lederer maintains, "are those relating to the reunion of Gerda and Kay.... [For] they show us how lonely we are or have been; how, if we are men, we need the validation, the confirmation, the redemption by women; and if we are women, how the redemption of such a lonely man is one of the magic feats, one of the miracles a woman can perform."[6] I do not agree entirely with Lederer. There may be a distinctively womanly way that Gerda sets out to save Kay. And we must discuss whether this is or is not gender-specific. But Lederer generalizes from this story in such a way that he seems to suggest that the role of redemptor belongs solely to woman. I want to say that the roles are interchangeable—and I think Andersen would agree with me. The wholeness of man and woman depends upon a relationship of complete mutuality.

But Lederer is right that the heart of evil is the cold heart of a self in isolation vainly imagining that by being autonomous it is free and whole. Some of the ways in which the differences between men and women are described by contemporary critics unfortunately only contribute suspicion, separation, and loneliness. Andersen's story is a healthy reminder that communion and love are the highest goals of human association. "As he [Kay] clung to her [Gerda]," writes Andersen, "the pieces of ice" that Kay had struggled with for all his time in captive isolation "danced for joy all round them, and where they grew tired lay down . . . [and] formed the very letters the Snow Queen had told him he must find out if he were to be his own master and she were to give him the whole world and a new pair of skates" (p. 269). The good that the Snow Queen abhors is not an abstract principle but the communion of love that heals the primal rift forced by Adam and Eve when they succumbed to the promise of an impossible twisted autonomy and immortality. In Hans Christian Andersen's *The Snow Queen*, goodness and immortality are rightly considered in relation to the communion in love that ought to exist between man and woman.

The Lion, the Witch and the Wardrobe: Diabolic Enchantment and the Liberation of Forgiveness

Like Hans Christian Andersen, C. S. Lewis explores the dynamism of evil that immobilizes and destroys our humanity and forcefully depicts the struggle between good and evil that is waged within the human heart. His story *The Lion, the Witch and the Wardrobe*, the first of the Narnia series, embraces the great themes of sin, repentance, and forgiveness in the Christian story of salvation.

Like Kay, Edmund Pevensie, the youngest of the four brothers and sisters who visit Narnia, does not consciously set out to be evil. Youthful pride, sibling rivalry, and jealousy are the only imperfections that evil needs in order to capture his youthful imagination, twist his mind, and set him on a disastrous course from which he will need to be rescued by another. The rescuer, in this case, is Aslan, the great Lion, the son of the Emperor-Beyond-the-Sea. Alsan is the long-looked-for Messiah of Narnian faith who will come to redeem the land from its captivity in a perpetual winter under the rule of the White Witch, who is Queen of Narnia.

Kathryn Lindskoog helps to confirm my own long-held suspicion that there is a connection between Andersen's story and Lewis's. In a book entitled *The Lion of Judah in Never-Never Land*, she astutely observes:

> Edmund's encounter with the witch, which leads to his enchantment, is parallel to the story of little Kay meeting the evil snow queen. . . . Both of these witches appear in great sledges, dressed in white fur. Both are tall and beautiful and seem always perfect to the eyes of their little victims; both are as cold and pale as white snow. As soon as the boys are enchanted, they are no longer afraid. They feel very important, try to show off, and indiscreetly tell anything that is asked of them.[7]

Lindskoog concludes that in both stories an evil antagonist appeals to a young boy's self-centeredness and pride and inordinate desire for some *thing* and gains a demonic control over him.

The Story and Edmund's Place in It

The Lion, the Witch and the Wardrobe is a fantasy and a morality play that captures the imaginations of children because it so closely reflects their own experiences of, and feelings about belonging to a family, sharing a life with siblings, and the difficulty of controlling passions and appetites. At the start, Lewis introduces his reader to the four Pevensie children, who in this and other books journey into the parallel world of Narnia. A dramatic struggle between good and evil is being played out in Narnia, a struggle much like that described in the Christian saga of creation, fall, and redemption. Upon their arrival in Narnia, the four children are told by Mr. and Mrs. Beaver that when four sons and daughters of Adam enter Narnia this is the sign that Aslan is returning to reclaim his kingdom. Then he will hand over his reign to them, making them kings and queens of

Narnia, who will rule from the thrones that await them at the ancient castle of Cair Paravel.

Lucy, the youngest of the children, enters Narnia before the others. She is a child of uncommon innocence and also deep intuition, who seems especially drawn to mystery. Susan, the second oldest, is tender-hearted but timid and normally falters when faced with the unknown. Peter is the oldest of the Pevensie children. He is courageous and rises to become the High King of Narnia sharing his reign with his three younger siblings.

But Edmund's role in this story is special, and is the focal point of the story, apart from the character of Aslan himself. For Edmund is "the prodigal" and the "most important of the children to the theme of redemption." Like Kay in *The Snow Queen*, Edmund is not what we would call a great sinner. Rather, "he is a small boy whose tendency to selfishness and bullying needs to be checked before it colors his whole life."[8] Like Kay, he is everyman or, to be more exact, everyboy. Edmund has too much pride, and this pride gets in the way of his better judgment. On Lucy's second journey into Narnia, Edmund follows her through the mysterious wardrobe. When he encounters the White Witch, for the first time, he does "not like the way she looked at him."[9] But he does not follow his better judgment and turn away from her. Instead, he lets down his guard and submits to her charm. He takes the deadly bait she dangles in front of him and falls entirely under her spell. Edmund (like Kay) becomes mentally confused: his mind becomes the captive of its own prison of "fallacious ratonalization."[10]

Edmund's pride and desire to shine above his siblings

aid and abet his desire to believe the White Witch's promise that if he brings his brother and sisters to her, she, in turn, will make him the Prince and—later on—the King of all Narnia. We do not know whether the witch has ever before encountered a human child, but she certainly figures out quickly how to hold Edmund's attention, capture his will, and pry into his mind. Hunger is perhaps the most powerful bodily and emotional force that can influence and change the behavior of a small child. Physical appetite, combined with a strong sense of taste, can literally overwhelm a child with dizzying desire. When Edmund comes upon the White Witch for the first time, he is disoriented, cold, and *hungry*. The witch magically produces a cup of hot tea and then asks Edmund what he would like to eat. He answers, "Turkish Delight, please, your Majesty." Then the Queen produces a box "tied with a green silk ribbon . . . [that] contain several pounds of" the candy (p. 38). Edmund hurriedly consumes all of it as he becomes entirely fixated on this source of such a strong pleasure in the midst of a very unpleasant and frightening situation. He no longer is cold or afraid. This enables the Queen to pry from him all the information she needs to make her plans to thwart the prophecy of the end of her power over Narnia. Lewis writes:

> At first Edmund tried to remember that it is rude to speak with one's mouth full, but he soon forgot about this and thought only of trying to shovel down as much Turkish Delight as he could, and the more he ate the more he wanted to eat, and he never asked himself why the Queen should be so inquisitive. (p. 38)

Lewis accurately portrays a common childhood experience of aching hunger and the insatiable and uncontrollable need to "fill the stomach" and satisfy taste. Edmund's behavior is wholly believable and existentially compelling for young people. They can relate to the vortexlike inner force that swallows him up into his dark night and descent into a personal hell. Edmund's hunger is a metaphor, also, for a deeper form of desire that draws not only children but also adults into sin and evil.

Gilbert Meilaender identifies the source of Edmund's religious and moral crisis. "The key to the understanding of evil in Lewis's story," writes Meilaender, "is given to us" in the phrase "the more he ate the more he wanted to eat. At that moment Edmund wants nothing more than he wants Turkish Delight; and his inordinate love makes a god of Turkish Delight, a god that leads him on and controls him."[11] All of the White Witch's future power over Edmund is predicated on this inordinate love. Edmund's defiance leads to a self-imposed alienation from his own siblings. And this encounter with the White Witch and the taste of her forbidden food marks the start of his long lonely journey into the darkness. In his twisted and confused mind, his brother and sisters grow ugly and insignificant, so that he cannot even understand why the Queen would want to bother with them. Nevertheless, Edmund decides that he will bring his brother and sisters back to the witch as she demands. Thus, evil takes a foothold in Edmund's will and imagination, much like the rot that attacks the soft spot of a fruit and spreads through the entire flesh. Whatever else Edmund does, even to hurt his brother and sisters, he rationalizes in terms of some greater good that he persuades himself he sees better than they can. He convinces himself that all the bad things said about the White Witch are untrue. Later he says to himself, "All these people who say nasty things about her are her enemies and probably half of it isn't true. She was jolly nice to me, anyway, much nicer than they are. I expect she is the rightful Queen really" (pp. 96–97).

After the Queen leaves him, Edmund and Lucy are reunited. She straightforwardly tells Edmund that she has learned of an evil White Witch who is holding Narnia in her thrall. Edmund realizes that his sister is referring to the person he has met but keeps his encounter with the Queen secret so as not to have to face the truth about his own treacherous heart or admit that Lucy is right. Even small children can relate to this manner of self-deception. They know just what Edmund is up to.

Following their return to the everyday world, Edmund denies to the others that he was ever with Lucy in Narnia. But he cannot get his mind off the Turkish Delight. Lewis wants us to think of sin as a kind of addiction. Some adults in continuing education courses that I have taught, who have had spouses with substance addictions or worked with alcoholics and drug addicts, have remarked that Edmund shows all the signs of the addict. In any case, Edmund's temptation becomes an uncontrolled obsession and he is no longer able to enjoy good and legitimate pleasures, much as with Kay, everything that is truly beautiful looks ugly.

Edmund's act of complete treachery follows. When all four of the children enter Narnia together they are led to the home of the good Beavers. The Beavers are among the remnant of Narnians who still believe in the ancient prophecy that Narnia will be liberated. At dinner Edmund's desire for the poisonous food of the White Witch overwhelms him.

> He had eaten his share of the dinner, but he hadn't really enjoyed it because he was thinking all the time about the Turkish Delight—and there's nothing that spoils the taste of good ordinary food half so much as the memory of bad magic food. (p. 95)

The Beavers relate the history of Narnia. But when Mr. Beaver gets to the part about Aslan and the plan to meet him in the appointed place in order to fulfill the ancient prophecies, Edmund makes up his mind to slip away and go to the witch's castle with the information. "For the mention of Aslan gave him a mysterious and horrible feeling just as it gave the others a mysterious and lovely feeling." Edmund makes a bad decision. Nevertheless, admonishes Lewis, "You mustn't think that even now Edmund was quite so bad that he actually wanted his brother and sisters to be turned into stone. . . . He managed to believe, or to pretend he believed, that she wouldn't do anything very bad to them" (p. 96). Edmund may be getting himself and the others into serious trouble, but he is still redeemable.

The Way to Goodness after the Fall: Repentance and Forgiveness

Evan Gibson observes that the story of *The Lion, the Witch and the Wardrobe* centers on Aslan: he is the "unifying character of the entire [Narnia] series."[12] The expectation of the lion's reappearance, his arrival, his sacrificial act that saves the life of Edmund, and his resurrection that seals the liberation of Narnia are the dramatic heart of the story. The scene when Aslan willingly submits to being bound and permits his great mane to be shorn, followed by his voluntary death, is a moving depiction of self-donative love. In order to save Edmund, Aslan must offer his own life in the boy's stead, since blood is the currency of sacrifice and salvation.

If we concentrate too much on these memorable moments, however, we risk overlooking the vital struggle between good and evil that is waged in Edmund's heart and reaches a conclusion even before this occurance at the story's close. This struggle within Edmund and its final outcome speak powerfully to children. Children see that, while it is difficult, admitting one's mistakes and errors is the right thing to do and may lead to forgiveness and true happiness.

Edmund comes to regret his decision to seek out the White Witch. But at the start, his plunge into darkness and ignominy seems irreversible. Propelled by his insatiable appetite for the witch's poisonous food and driven by his pride and spitefulness, Edmund is in a free fall into darkness and void. "The silence and the loneliness were dreadful." In his narrator's voice, Lewis comments, "In fact I really think he might have given up the whole plan and gone back and owned up and made friends with the others, if he hadn't happened to say to himself, 'When I'm King of Narnia the first thing I shall do will be to make some decent roads.'" The diabolical imagination has some things in common with the moral imagination. It too has its alluring landscapes and objects of delight. And so Edmund begins to imagine how as king "he would make laws against beavers and dams . . . and . . . schemes for keeping Peter in his place" (p. 98).

When he arrives at the gates of the Queen's castle,

Edmund even manages to overcome fear that might ordinarily have turned him around. Initially, he is terrorized by the sight of a stone lion that he thinks is Aslan. But he quickly realizes that the lion is a statue and decides that the White Witch has transformed Aslan into stone as she does with all of her enemies that she takes prisoner. In a spiteful act of feigned courage, he defaces the lion by penciling in a mustache over its lips and drawing a pair of spectacles around its eyes. But the beast, writes Lewis, still looked "so terrible, and sad, and noble, staring up in the moonlight that Edmund didn't really get any fun out of jeering" (p. 103). Once again Lewis hints that Edmund's heart is not entirely hardened. Kay's transformation back to his better self is virtually instantaneous, once it is warmed and awakened by the tears and tender embrace of Gerda. Perhaps in these moments of fear and isolation the same is possible for Edmund, but he is not visited by such an angel. Edmund's dark journey has only begun, and he will travel it alone until the appointed hour.

Finally, after encountering countless stone statues of every kind of Narnian creature, Edmund is greeted by the White Witch. Her displeasure that he has not brought his siblings with him and her alarm at the news that Aslan may be on the move, spell misery for Edmund. She refuses to give him more Turkish Delight. Instead he gets a bowl of water and a plate of dry bread. Then he is loaded onto the witch's sledge as they race to cut off Aslan at the sacred Stone Table. Lewis describes Edmund's dreadful situation.

> This was a terrible journey for Edmund who had no coat. Before they had been going a quarter of an

> hour all the front of him was covered with snow. . . . Soon he was wet to the skin. And oh, how miserable he was! It didn't look now as if the Witch intended to make him a King! All the things he had said to make himself believe that she was good and kind and that her side was really the right side sounded to him silly now. (p. 124)

The nightmare still gets worse. After what seems like an eternity, the sledge comes upon a family of squirrels, some satyrs, a dwarf, and an old dog-fox who are having a picnic party because Father Christmas has returned to Narnia and the perpetual winter without Christmas is ending. The witch knows that this means that her spell is being broken by a power greater than her own. And over Edmund's pleas of "Oh don't, don't, please don't," (p. 127) she waves her wand and turns them all into statues. Once the terrible deed is done, the witch strikes Edmund hard on the face and says, "Let that teach you to ask favor for spies and traitors" (p. 128). Lewis now interjects, "And Edmund for the first time in this story felt sorry for someone besides himself." Having come so near to being turned into a statue himself, or perhaps even fearing that the same would befall him soon, empathy and pity now shift his imaginings to the dreadful meaning of such a fate. "It seemed so pitiful to think of those little stone figures sitting there all the silent days and all the dark nights, year after year, till the moss grew on them and at last even their faces crumbled away" (p. 128).

Edmund feels compassion. And compassion is a powerful impulse in the human breast. It has deep, even physiological resonances. It comes from the very "guts" of our being. It taps a primal sense that we are all bound one to another in a solidarity of flesh and spirit. Compassion binds us especially to the suffering of others so that we share their suffering vicariously and want to do something to alleviate it. No one who is without compassion deserves forgiveness. But he who has compassion is already far along toward repentance. Compassion not only awakens us to the suffering of others but moves us to see how we are responsible for having brought some of that suffering about. This movement of compassion and the dynamic of forgiveness are at the heart of the story of the two thieves crucified beside Jesus. One thief heaps scorn upon the Man. "Are you not the Messiah? Save yourself and us." But the other rebukes him, "Do you not fear God, since you are under the same sentence of condemnation? And indeed we have been condemned justly, for we are getting what we deserve for our deeds, but this man has done nothing wrong." He then says to Jesus, "Remember me when you come into your kingdom." And Jesus replies, "Truly I tell you, today you will be with me in Paradise" (Luke 23:39–43 RSV).

Gradually, just as the snow that covers Narnia begins to melt, Edmund's heart turns back to goodness. In the old religious language, Edmund is converted. Lewis himself insisted that he did not set out to write an allegory of the Christian gospel of redemption. He preferred to describe *The Lion, the Witch and the Wardrobe* as a story that runs parallel to the gospel, as if in the story it were being asked, "What if the Messiah were to come in another world?" This may be so. But the story of Edmund communicates religious and moral truths that are inseparable from the teachings about sin and redemption in the Bible. Evil in Narnia, as in the Bible, is fundamentally a rebellion against the deity. Evil is vanquished in the human soul when the person turns against his own pride and selfishness back toward God. That turn may well begin in the compassionate act of loving the suffering other as one would love oneself.

When Edmund is finally saved from the clutches of the White Witch, he has already undergone an inner transformation. When Aslan takes him aside and presumably reminds him of his wrongdoings and the great trouble his treachery has wrought, Edmund is already penitent. And so everything can be forgiven and forgotten. "There is no need to tell you (and no one ever heard) what Aslan was saying, but it was a conversation which Edmund never forgot. As the others drew nearer Aslan turned to meet them bringing Edmund with him. 'Here is your brother,' he said, 'and—there is no need to talk to him about what is past.'" Then Edmund turns to the others and says "'I'm sorry,' and everyone said 'That's all right'" (pp. 152–53). The circle of sin, repentance, and forgiveness is completed. Later in the battle that brings about the final victory, Edmund proves his worthiness. "He had become his real old self again and could look you in the face" (p. 197). And in the future Edmund is called "King Edmund the Just" (p. 201).

Conclusion

The stories of Kay in *The Snow Queen* and Edmund in *The Lion, the Witch and the Wardrobe* are similar. And yet there are also important differences. Kay's innocence seems more pristine and his suffering less deserved than Edmund's. Andersen raises difficult questions about the phenomenon of affliction, of being the unsuspecting and undeserving victim of evil. Yet we actually learn very little about Kay's inner state during his imprisonment in the Snow Queen's frozen palace. And Kay's redemption happens almost as suddenly as his capture. Most of the story is about Gerda and her untiring quest to find and be reunited with her beloved Kay. Andersen tells his story primarily from the point of view of the lover and redeemer who will not abandon the beloved in his distress. It is from Gerda's experiences that we come to realize the vicious blow that evil strikes at love and communion in life.

Lewis, on the other hand, takes great pains to describe the evolution of Edmund's inner state of mind and heart as he grows more and more wedded to the evil that he has met. Edmund is young, though perhaps not quite as young as Kay, and he like Kay is also a victim of a temptress. But unlike Kay, Edmund is truly culpable. And so whereas Andersen tells a profound and haunting tale about the genesis of evil, the inscrutable and unpredictable thing that it is, and the brokenness it inflicts upon life, Lewis's story is about what biblical religion calls sin, the willful rejection of goodness and the willing embrace of evil. It is also about repentance, rejection of that very same evil, and thus its disarmament from the human will and imagination. And last of all, *The Lion, the Witch and the Wardrobe* is about redemption—the conversion of the mind and rescue of the heart by the Divine Lover who never gives up on the beloved and forgives the beloved unconditionally.

6

Heroines of Faith and Courage: Princess Irene in *The Princess and the Goblin* and Lucy in *Prince Caspian*

George MacDonald's *The Princess and the Goblin* was published in 1872 and was followed some nine years later (in 1881) by a sequel, *The Princess and Curdie*. The protagonists of these fairy-tale romances are two of the most memorable children in Victorian literature—the Princess Irene and the miner's son Curdie.

In this chapter, I will deal only with *The Princess and the Goblin* and the character of the Princess Irene. One other character, aside from the boy Curdie, figures prominently in this discussion. She is the mysterious great-great-grandmother whom Irene discovers one day in the attic rooms of her home. The grandmother is a numinous presence in the story, a type of wise woman or wisdom figure that MacDonald introduced into a number of his more well-known fantasies. Through the relationship that develops between the grandmother and Irene, MacDonald builds tissue and membrane into the faith and courage of his young heroine.

The Role of the Moral Imagination in George MacDonald's Storytelling

I for one can really testify to a book that has made a difference to my whole existence, which helped me to see things in a certain way from the start; a vision of things which even so real a revelation as a change of religious allegiance has substantially only crowned and confirmed. Of all the stories I have read, including even all the novels of the same novelist, it remains the most real, the most life like. It is called The Princess and the Goblin, *and is by George MacDonald.*

G. K. Chesterton

There are critics who say that George MacDonald wrote over the heads of children. MacDonald himself said that he wrote for "children" of all ages. He endeavored to appeal to the childlike in everyone—not the childish, but the *childlike*—and to feed the moral imagination. MacDonald did not exaggerate the power of the imagination. Imagination is a power of discovery, not a power to create. The latter capacity he reserved to God alone. Nor did MacDonald equate imagination with mere fancy, what we used to call "vain imaginings." Rather, for him, imagination is a power of perception, a light that illumines the mystery that is hidden beneath visible reality: it is a power to help "see" into the very nature of things. Reason alone, MacDonald argued, is not able to recognize mystery or grasp the moral quiddity of the world. As the sensible mind needs eyes to see, so reason needs the imagination in order to behold mystery and to perceive the true quality of things. Imagination takes reason to the threshold of mystery and moral truth and reveals them as such. Reason may then approve or submit. But it remains for the heart of courage with the will to believe and the vision of imagination to embrace the beauty of goodness and the strength of truth as the foundation of virtuous living.

MacDonald advised parents: "Seek not that your sons and your daughters should not see visions, should not dream dreams; seek that they should see true visions, that they should dream noble dreams."[1] But a literature that would awaken the imagination with such effect is bound to outpace the dull-witted adult every bit as much as the child whose mind is the captive of a utilitarian education that teaches nothing but "the facts."

George MacDonald dared to invent a modern genre of fairy tale that even today challenges the positivism and twisted puritanism of our contemporary taste for stories "suited" for children. He eschewed both the popular penchant for so-called practical stories about "real life" and the untrained appetite for sentimental stories suffused with warm feelings. Why shouldn't children's stories arouse deep questionings about the nature of good and evil, about death and what comes after, and about faith and doubt? Do we not risk doing much greater harm to our children if we deny them the opportunities and the possibilities to work through their fears, inquire into the meaning of their loves, and follow the lead of questions about the human lot that begin to percolate to consciousness quite early in life?

The Princess and the Goblin is a story that breathes with this freedom and risk. It is a story about a young girl of just eight years, who, although she is a real princess, "grows up" very fast to become a *real* woman. And it begins when, as I have mentioned, Irene discovers in the attic of the house in which she lives a mysterious woman who is both old and young and beautiful and frightening, and whose love, as Irene also learns, spares not pain.

How Faith and Courage Need One Another in *The Princess and the Goblin*

We teach everyone and instruct everyone in all the ways of wisdom, so as to present each one of you as a mature member of Christ's body.

Colossians 1:28 NEB

But you are a chosen race, a royal priesthood, a dedicated nation, a people claimed by God for his own . . . called . . . out of darkness into his marvellous light.

Peter 2:9 NEB

"The princess was a sweet little creature, and at the time my story begins, was about eight years old, I think, *but she got older very fast*" (my emphasis) (p. 5). This is how George MacDonald introduces his reader to the young heroine, Princess Irene; and with the simple and easily overlooked phrase "*but she got older very fast*" also plants the first and most significant clue about the meaning and nature of Irene's relationship with her mysterious grandmother.

At the start of the story, we are told that the Princess Irene does not live with her father the king in his palace. Instead, she lives in "a large house, half castle, half farm-house" in the countryside on the side of a mountain (p. 5). This is because her mother was not strong when Irene was born and we are also given to suspect that the mother is deceased at the time the story begins. But danger lurks beneath the mountain on which the house rests. Inside the mountain resides a race of goblins who hold an ancient grudge against the king and his family and are set on a plan to capture Irene and marry her to Harelip, the goblin crown-prince.

The king is aware of the presence of these creatures, and so Irene is watched carefully. She is not permitted to go out after dark because the goblins sometimes venture to the surface at night and cause mischief. The king is unaware, however, of the goblin's scheme to take his daughter prisoner. It remains for a boy named Curdie, who works with his father in the mines, to discover the goblin plan and finally to foil it. Meanwhile, the story's main action shifts back and forth from "the universal and constant darkness" (p. 100) of the goblin dwellings below, where Curdie pursues his mission, to the grandmother's moon-and-starlit garret rooms that Irene visits.

But let us start at the beginning. One dreary day when she is unhappily closed up in her nursery, Irene slips into a deep slumber. When she awakens, she falls from her chair hard onto the floor. Then, for no apparent reason at all, the little princess races out of the nursery, dashes in a direction she has not gone before, and scampers up "a curious old stair" (p. 9) which leads to she knows not where.[2] A child (even an adult reader) might wonder whether Irene is really quite awake or whether she is in a dream—later Irene herself wonders the same. Irene's inexhaustible curiosity (signified by the play on words, "curious stairs"), sends her upstairs until she reaches a landing where she follows a narrow hall lined with doors, all of which are closed shut. The rapping of the rain on the roof disturbs Irene and she hurries to find the stairs to the safety of her nursery. She is unsuccessful and runs crying down the labyrinthine corridors. But Irene does not cry for long, MacDonald interjects, because she is "brave as could be expected of a princess of her age" (p. 9).

Irene collects herself and resolves once more to find her way back to her nursery. But she only gets more lost and now becomes quite afraid. She reaches another flight of stairs that lead up only. With no other choice left to her, Irene scrambles up these stairs until, at last, she arrives at a small square landing with three doors, one to either side and a third facing her. She hesitates at first, not sure "what to do next." Then all of a sudden, she hears "a curious humming sound. . . . It was . . . like the hum of a very happy bee that had found a rich well of honey in some globular flower." The sound is coming from behind the door in front of her. Irene opens it, and there in full view is "a very old lady" seated at a spinning wheel (p. 11).

This is a suspenseful moment. The first time I read *The Princess and the Goblin* to my son Rafi he was about Irene's age, and he stopped me and asked nervously: "Is the old lady good or bad?" Only with great hesitancy did he let me continue. My daughter Victoria asked the same question when I read the story to her; but she would not even permit me to read further unless I assured her that the lady would do no harm to Irene. Perhaps because of his extraordinary oral storytelling powers, which he practiced on his own children, MacDonald was remarkably good at intoning a voice in his writing that stirs the emotions and arouses a sense of awe. Yet sometimes fear and awe are not so easily disentangled, as testified by the responses of my son and daughter.

I think that MacDonald makes Irene's first adventure

up the stairs into a metaphor for a process wherein the self (in this case Irene, or any child) is challenged by its most primal fears to risk safety in order to learn more and be in command of one's own powers. When Irene runs down the stairs thinking she has found her way back to her "safe nursery," MacDonald adds enigmatically: "So she thought, but she had lost herself long ago. It doesn't follow that she *was* lost, because she had lost herself, though" (p. 9).

In a short space, the reader learns better what this action signifies. Having been magically returned by her grandmother to her nursery room, Irene tells a disbelieving nanny where she has been and whom she has discovered in the garret rooms at the top of the house. She is bothered when her nurse suggests that perhaps she was dreaming, and bursts out: "I didn't dream it. I went upstairs, and I lost myself, and if I hadn't found the beautiful lady, I should never have found myself" (p. 18). Irene couldn't possibly intend the deeper meaning that MacDonald invests in her words. But he is playing deliberately on the biblical theme of losing one's life in order to gain it (Matt. 10:39), of following Christ, even to death, and by so doing becoming a true daughter or son of God. Irene's belief in her grandmother and willingness to obey her, launch her on an important journey toward moral and spiritual maturity—a passage by trial that calls on her to risk even her life in order to save the life of another.

MacDonald's careful portrait of the grandmother and her environs also deserves attention. The great-great-grandmother is no ordinary person and Irene's complete entrustment of herself into the mysterious woman's care and guidance is analogous to a religious act of giving oneself over to something or someone sacred and transcendent. The grandmother is quite beautiful, although in a most unusual way. Her skin is "smooth and white," and her hair, which is "combed back from her forehead and face," hangs loose "far down and all over her back." She would not appear to be old, except that her eyes look "so wise that you could not have helped seeing she must be old." And her hair is "white almost as snow" (p. 11). Moonlight floods the rooms that the woman inhabits and the walls are painted blue, "spangled all over with what looked like stars of silver" (p. 64). On one occasion the woman herself is dressed in "slippers [that] glimmer with the light of the milky way, for they were covered with seed-pearls and opals in one mass" (p. 79).

In every respect, the grandmother is surrounded in mystery, literally clothed with numinous qualities, so that some commentators have associated her with the ancient Greek goddess Demeter, the daughter of Cronos and Rhea, sister of Zeus.[3] In my view, the striking symbolism of the blue sky, the moon, and the stars suggests more strongly Christian meaning—namely, the person of the Virgin Mary. Traditionally, with just such symbolism, Mary is represented in Christian art and poetry as the Queen of Heaven.[4]

MacDonald leads the reader still more deeply into the mystery of the grandmother's identity and Irene's relationship to her. Yes, the old woman tells Irene that she is her great-great-grandmother, that she is a queen herself, that her name is Irene also, and that, indeed, Irene is named after her (pp. 13, 14). But a spiritual bond unites the two that transcends even the implied biological relationship and family connection. At the start of the story, MacDonald describes Irene's face as "fair and pretty, with eyes [just] like two bits of night sky, each with a star dissolved in the blue. . . . Those eyes you would have thought must have known they came from [the sky], so often were they turned up in that direction" (p. 5). And Irene's own bedroom nursery ceiling is painted "blue, with stars in it" (p. 5), *just like the grandmother's.*

Thus, it seems that when Irene discovers the grandmother and entrusts herself to the woman, Irene is finding her own deepest identity and destiny. Contemporary interpreters have interpreted this process in purely psychological terms.[5] They point not only to the correspondences of imagery in the descriptions of Irene and the grandmother and their surroundings but to several other scenes in order to argue that this is a story about a young girl's passage from childhood to puberty, individuation, and psychological self-integration.

One such scene occurs in Irene's nursery the evening that she visits the grandmother for a second time. Irene pricks her thumb on a brooch and her thumb bleeds a drop of blood. Irene falls asleep, but the swelling and pain eventually awaken her and she follows the bright moonlight that is streaming through the windows up the old oak stairs to the grandmother's rooms. The spot of blood and the lunar imagery have been interpreted as alluding to the female menstrual cycle, so that the phrase "she got older very fast" means that Irene was about to make her passage into adolescence.

But I disagree. I do not think that this is what MacDonald had in mind at all. We live in an age that is obsessed with supposed psychological and sexual connotations of words and actions, whereas MacDonald's "obsession" was over spiritual matters. This means his theological convictions need to be taken seriously. (And, after all, eight years old does seem a bit young for the onset of puberty.) MacDonald stations a strong metaphor at the heart of this story—as witnessed by the title itself. Princess is the root metaphor in his story, and I believe it is the key to the meaning in the images and events that have been mentioned. Furthermore, it explains the primary significance of Irene's relationship to the grandmother.

For in biblical faith, princess, like king or queen, has sacral and sacramental connotations: it signifies a divine calling to moral responsibility and spiritual leadership. Irene's spiritual "rite of passage" under the direction and care of the mysterious and numinous grandmother carries this kind of sacral and sacramental meaning. In the magazine version of the story, MacDonald interrupts the narrative with this revealing dialogue between the "Editor" and an imaginary reader:

> "But Mr. Editor, why do you always write about princesses?"
>
> "Because every little girl is a princess."
>
> "You will make them vain if you tell them that."
>
> "Not if they understand what I mean."
>
> "Then what do you mean?"
>
> "What do you mean by a princess?"
>
> "The daughter of a king."
>
> "Very well; then every little girl is a princess, and there would be no need to say anything about it except that she is always in danger of forgetting her rank."[6]

So MacDonald is quite clear about this. He reminds us of the several levels of meaning of princess. But he wants us to ponder especially its religious meaning for which the earthly political and social title is only a metaphor. To be a princess means ultimately to claim a status as a child of God the Father (and perhaps Mary, the Queen of Heaven, if I have read MacDonald accurately) and to become a full member of the household of God. How one achieves this status is what his story is really about. And faith and courage are strongly associated with this special identity and calling. Together they are virtues that have the power to open our lives onto the mystery of our relationship as sons and daughters of God.

The Trial and Transformation of Princess Irene

There is no fear in love, but perfect love casts out fear . . . and whoever fears has not reached perfection in love.

1 John 4:18 RSV

Courage is one of the cardinal virtues named by the great classical and Christian thinkers of Western culture. Plato, Aristotle, Cicero, and Thomas Aquinas all agree that courage is the moral and spiritual capacity to risk harm or danger to oneself for the sake of something good. And yet not one of these writers maintains that courage banishes fear entirely—although it certainly is the opposite of cowardice. If these authorities are right about courage, then our modern dictionaries can be misleading.

For example, a widely used school dictionary, which I purchased for my son and daughter when they were in grade school, defines courage as "a quality that makes it possible for a person to face danger or difficulties *without fear* (my emphasis)."[7] In *The Princess and the Goblin*, MacDonald agrees with the ancient authorities and dissents from the modern dictionary. We cannot fully understand the process of Irene's maturation into the full status of a "princess" unless we see how courage and fear are related in her character and how, in the end, her faith fortifies her courage, enabling her to conquer her fear and make her a strong daughter of the "King."

On her second visit with her great-great-grandmother, Irene exclaims: "I don't think you are ever afraid of anything." And the woman replies: "Not for long, at least, my child. Perhaps by the time I am two thousand years of age, I shall, indeed, never be afraid of anything. But I confess I have sometimes been afraid about my children—sometimes about you, Irene" (p. 86). A fear for one's own safety and the well-being of others that arises from the rich soil of our humanity and the relationships we forge in life is perfectly natural, says MacDonald. It is the reasonable response of a rational being to something that endangers those relationships. It is like a pain in the body which signifies that a limb or an organ might come to harm. Fear, like physical pain, signals the need for preventive measures and a remedy. Courage may be that remedy.

MacDonald also demonstrates that courage and fear are paradoxically related. They share fundamental things in common and yet they point to very different outcomes. Both arise from the same deep wellsprings of our human condition. Both originate in our creaturely finiteness and our mortal nature as well as from our capacity and our need to love and be loved. Both are psychologically and spiritually counterpoised to death. Unlike fear, however, courage enables us to stand fast in the face of danger, not to waver or flee from it, but instead to thwart danger, before it brings harm to us or to others.

Nevertheless, Irene's suspicion that her grandmother

knows no fear is not entirely groundless. The difference that Irene sees in her grandmother is that while the mysterious woman may experience moments of fear for others, she no longer fears for herself. The grandmother's fear for her "children" is connected to love like muscle is to the tendon. Fear and love work together within her so that love sublimates fear into the courage to be and to act for the good of her children.

Indeed, MacDonald believed that fear is a precondition of as well as a force that drives toward moral and spiritual perfection. The grandmother alludes to this perfection when she says to Irene that maybe in two thousand years even she, who is so fearless and beautiful in Irene's eyes, will outgrow fear entirely—much as the saints "outgrow" sin in their constant struggle to become holy. In a sermon, MacDonald explained this concept:

> Fear is natural, and has a part to perform nothing but itself could perform in the birth of the true humanity. Until love, which is the truth towards God, is able to cast out fear, it is well that fear should hold; it is a bond, however poor, between that which is and that which creates, a bond that must be broken only by the tightening of an infinitely closer bond.[8]

MacDonald believed that the height of fear is also its transcendent focal point. Biblical religion speaks of this fear as the "fear of God." And when all of our common fears are successfully referred to this one "fear," then all that are left are love and obedience to God. Thus,

MacDonald distinguished between our common fears and the fear of the Holy. The former challenges the self to face and overcome the existential reasons that give rise to fear, the possibilities of personal diminishment and death. The latter perfects the courage that the common variety of fear demands of the self. And it transforms this fear into a bridge to complete obedience to God. "Obedience is but the other side of the creative will. Will is God's will, obedience is man's will: the two make one," MacDonald observed.[9] And he went on to make this significant religious statement:

> The Root-Life, knowing well the thousand troubles it would bring upon Him, has created, and goes on creating other lives, that, though incapable of self-being, they may, by willed obedience, share in the bliss of His essential self-ordained being. If we do the will of God, eternal life is ours—no mere continuity of existence, for that in itself is worthless as hell, but a being that is one with essential Life, and so within His reach to fill with the abundant and endless outgoing of His love.[10]

Courage, therefore, is an important natural virtue that helps us to navigate a course to the supernatural end of perfection through obedience to God. All of the so-called natural virtues, including courage, are profoundly related to the cardinal theological virtues of faith, hope, and love through a ceaseless and heightening process of participation in the goodness and immortality of the Divine Life.

Irene's maturation takes this course as she learns to

trust in her grandmother and follow her instructions. Irene's courage, like all natural courage, comes from the struggle with fear. But courage also needs the ground of ultimate trust on which to stand and act—something or someone who embodies goodness and truth wholly and unqualifiedly. Then it may deepen into a courage to be wholly for others and to risk the self in their behalf. Authentic courage, therefore, makes use of faith and love, or, rather it fulfills itself in faith and love through selfless and unselfish acts of being for others. True to this conviction, MacDonald in *The Princess and the Goblin* shows us how courage gets joined with the theological virtues, especially faith and love.

Irene's Final Test

As I have said, the main action of *The Princess and the Goblin* shifts back and forth (or should I say "up" and" down") from the luminous garret rooms, where Irene visits her grandmother, to the dark mine shafts and dwellings of the goblins beneath the mountain, where Curdie unravels their plans to kidnap the princess. Irene journeys just once into the dark underworld inside the mountain. It is, however, the turning point of the story.

Her journey begins early one morning when she is awakened by the hideous noise of goblins outside her nursery window. Irene remembers the instructions her grandmother gave her that if she ever thought she was in grave danger, she must immediately remove her grandmother's ring from her finger and place it under her pillow. With the same ring finger she must feel for the gossamer thread spun for her by her grandmother that is attached to the ring. She then must follow the thread wherever it leads her, even if that be to the most unexpected places.

So Irene does just what her grandmother has told her. She follows the thread, even when it takes her straight into the mountain through narrow and winding passages. All this time Irene does not know that Curdie is being held prisoner and that the thread is leading her to him. So as the passages become more narrow and dark, Irene grows frightened and nearly despairs. Her trust in her grandmother wins out, however. "She kept thinking more and more about her grandmother, and all that she had said" (p. 107), writes MacDonald. Her grandmother had said that she must never "doubt the thread" (p. 84) and to trust that it would return her to safety.

The thread eventually brings Irene to Curdie and, after a tussle with some goblins, they both are delivered from the mountain as the thread leads them to the grandmother's bedroom. However, the physical danger that Irene has faced is only the prelude to one final difficult lesson. Curdie has refused to believe Irene's story about the thread, since he can neither see nor feel it. When they arrive at the garret, Curdie is also unable to see the grandmother or the beautiful furnishings of her bedroom. By his own testimony all that he can see is "a big, bare, garret-room—like the one in mother's cottage" (p. 121). Worse still for Irene, he is angry with her because he thinks that she has lied to him and has deliberately humiliated him.

The child in each one of us expects to be able to share with friends our greatest joy. In her childlike innocence, Irene quite simply assumes that Curdie will see her grandmother and believe everything she has told him.

Instead, she learns the hard truth that we cannot make even those whom we love most believe as we believe, and that, if we truly love them, then we must permit them to come freely to that belief.[11]

How Irene "Got Older Very Fast"

Then she carried her to the side of the room. Irene wondered what she was going to do with her, but she asked no questions—only starting a little when she found that she was going to lay her in the large silver bath; for as she looked into it, again she saw no bottom, but the stars shining miles away, as it seemed, in a great blue gulf. Her hands closed involuntarily on the beautiful arms that held her, and that was all.

The Princess and the Goblin

When a disconcerted Curdie leaves the grandmother's room, Irene bursts into tears. She beseeches her: "What does it all mean, grandmother?" And the woman answers as only Wisdom can: "It means, my love, that I did not mean to show myself. Curdie is not yet able to believe some things. . . . Seeing is not believing—it is only seeing" (pp. 122–23).

Patience is the practical fruit of faith and is a natural ally of courage. For the time being, Irene must endure being alone in her faith and wait patiently for Curdie. "I see," she says to her grandmother. "So as Curdie can't help it, I will not be vexed with him, but just wait" (p. 123). When Irene "lets go" of Curdie, her trust in the grandmother gives life to a new form of courage within her. The philosopher Josef Pieper has called this "'mystic' fortitude."[12] Irene ceases fearing for Curdie, not because she no longer cares for him, but because she believes in someone who cares for him even more. Mystic fortitude is an attribute of the faithful self that abandons itself for the sake of the other, letting go of earthly fear and natural desire. Mystic fortitude is entrustment of oneself and the ones one loves entirely to God. "The self is given to us that we may sacrifice it," wrote MacDonald. "It is ours, that we, like Christ, may have somewhat to offer—not that we should torment it, but that we should deny it; not that we should cross it, but that we should abandon it utterly. Then it can no more vex us."[13]

In his fantasy stories, George MacDonald brilliantly uncovered and explored the vital premoral roots of the virtues and the vices. However, he also found metaphors and invented allegories to illuminate the transcendent fulfillment of the virtues in mystic love and communion with God. According to MacDonald, the process by which a human being attains full maturity includes not only psychological development and moral growth but religious conversion, and, finally, mystical participation in the Divine Life. Pieper connects mystic fortitude and the self's self-sacrifice to God with baptism. He writes: "The more strictly moral fortitude . . . reaches essentially beyond itself [in self-abandonment, the more it reaches] into the mystic order, which, . . . is nothing other than the perfect unfolding of the supernatural life that every Christian receives in baptism."[14]

In *The Princess and the Goblin,* MacDonald too turns to the symbolism of baptism in order to convey this meaning. I think that Irene's descent into the mountain and ascent to the surface and up to the grandmother's rooms anticipates a "baptismal" event that she now experiences. Earlier, Irene literally disappeared beneath the earth and then arose from this "grave" because she did not lose faith. This symbolic journey of death, descent into Hades, and rebirth is completed in the grandmother's apartment. Dirty, exhausted, and downcast, Irene collapses into the arms of her grandmother and permits the woman to immerse her in the large silver basin. Irene has looked into that basin's bottomless depths before, and seen in them "the sky and the moon and the stars" (p. 81), infinity itself. We are invited to consider: "What would it take for a child of Irene's age to overcome the natural fear of being plunged into such bottomless depths?"

> The lady pressed her once more to her bosom, saying—
>
> "Do not be afraid, my child."
>
> "No, grandmother," answered the princess, with a little gasp; and the next instant she sank in the clear cool water. When she opened her eyes, she saw nothing but a strange lovely blue all over and beneath and all about her. The lady and the beautiful room had vanished from her sight, and she seemed utterly alone. But instead of *being afraid, she felt more than happy—perfectly blissful* (my emphasis). (p. 124)

The paradoxical relationships of fear and faith and fear and courage are never wholly resolved in our temporal lives. Indeed "fear is better than no God," wrote MacDonald, "better than god made with hands. [At least] in . . . fear [lies] deep hidden the sense of the infinite."[15] While fear may sweep us into nothingness, it is also the condition under which a finite and sinful human being finds the faith and courage to yield herself up entirely to God. Baptism is an initiation into and the beginning of a whole new way of being, a way of being whose ultimate end is life unspoiled by fear and ripened instead by Love. Irene will no doubt fear again. But she has also embarked on a new life. Fear will never be quite the same: Love will see to that.

After she is drawn out of the water, Irene immediately catches the sweet scent of the burning roses in her grandmother's fireplace. Then the woman dresses Irene in her nightgown which she has cleansed in that fire so that it is now "as white as snow." When Irene stands up, she feels "as if she had been made over again. Every bruise and all weariness were gone, and her hands were soft and whole as ever" (p. 125). The "death" of her old (childish) self is completed in the grandmother's font. Irene arises a new being possessing faith and courage, a true princess and daughter of the "King." She *has* grown up very fast, as we have been told she would. On the very next day she takes command of the household. And the royal attendants quickly realize that Irene is changed and has grown into the stature of her royal title. "Up to this moment, they had all regarded her as little more than a baby" (p. 135). Irene's nurse, however, saw that "she was no longer a mere child, but wiser than her age would account for" (p. 137).

George MacDonald's religious imagination took over where his moral imagination left off. Or more precisely, his moral imagination was thoroughly interpenetrated by his religious vision. The Greek and Stoic ideals of virtue for virtue's sake did not suffice for him. That is why he made a "baptismal event" the penultimate event of this story. Beatitude transcends not only fear but the death that we fear and the courage that helps us to face it. Immortality, the permanent home of the grandmother—the Queen of Heaven—is the reward and the achievement of a life lived faithfully and courageously. This, it seems to me, is the crowning meaning of George MacDonald's marvelous allegory.

How Lucy Saw: The Power of Faith in C. S. Lewis's *Prince Caspian*

Jesus said, "It is for judgment that I have come into this world—to give sight to the sightless and to make blind those who see."

John 9:39 REB

In *The Princess and the Goblin*, George MacDonald defines the heart of the relationship of faith and courage and depicts how together they are able to bring the self to moral maturity and, ultimately, mystical participation in the life of the Spirit. In *Prince Caspian*, of Lewis's Narnia series, Lewis likewise attends to this theme of moral and spiritual maturation through faith and courage. Furthermore, he expands on several closely related subjects—namely, faith as a power of memory and perception, and courage as a virtue that enacts faith.

My pairing of MacDonald and Lewis is neither accidental nor incidental. George MacDonald was a strong religious and literary influence on C. S. Lewis. He readily acknowledged that MacDonald's fantasy literature made an indelible impression on his artistic and religious imagination. Lewis credited the Victorian writer with not only "convert[ing]," but even "baptiz[ing]" his "imagination." This, he said, did not happen at the first meeting. But there came a time in Lewis's journey from atheism to faith when he was "ready to hear from him [MacDonald] much that he could not have told me at the first meeting."[16] Lewis had searched for the essential truth in religion that, he thought, could be held onto after the mythic wrappings are removed. MacDonald's fantasy works persuaded him, however, that the moral and spiritual truth of religion is inextricably interwoven with the myth and the story so that it cannot be removed like the kernel from the husk. Lewis also realized that that quality in MacDonald's imaginative works that had always enchanted him "turned out to be the [actual] quality of the real universe, the divine, magical, terrifying, and ecstatic reality in which we live."[17]

In the end, MacDonald inspired Lewis to make his own attempts at writing fairy tales and fantasy stories. These endeavors bore fruit in the seven books of Narnia and his *Space Trilogy*. Thus, while I cannot prove conclusively that MacDonald's Princess Irene was the inspiration for Lewis's Lucy Pevensie, I am personally persuaded of a strong connection. The length of time that separates the publication of the books in which Irene and Lucy appear spans nearly a century. Yet it is possible, nay appropriate, to say that these two young girls are sisters in faith and courage, much as their respective authors were brothers in spirit.

Lucy's Spiritual Lineage

In one of his sermons, George MacDonald argues that "the highest condition of the human will is in sight . . . I say not the highest condition of the Human Being," he continues, "that surely lies in the Beatific Vision, in the sight of God. But the highest condition of the Human Will . . . is when, not seeing God, not seeming itself to grasp Him, at all, it yet holds Him fast."[18] Thus, when the grandmother says to Irene that "seeing is not believing—it is only seeing" (p. 123), she sounds a theme that not only resonates with the biblical irony in the passage I have cited from the Gospel of John but also with MacDonald's own truest thoughts about the nature and power of faith.

When we trust in our bodily eyes we see what we desire, and normally (in our sinful and spiritually immature condition) that which we immediately desire is not God. MacDonald agreed with the great medieval doctors of faith who diagnosed the human condition as afflicted with what they called the "concupiscence of the eyes," lustful eyes of sinful flesh. In the preceding chapter, we saw how Hans Christian Andersen depicted this condition through the powerful allegory of the Devil's splintered looking glass. Without people even knowing it, fragments of the glass get lodged in their eyes and hearts, thus distorting their feelings and perceptions. They may even regard that which is ugly as beautiful and be drawn to wickedness rather than to goodness.

Nevertheless, while not all seeing is believing, believing is still a form of "seeing." Or putting the matter somewhat differently, one *truly* "sees" when one believes. When one believes, then the scales fall from one's eyes and one "sees" into the deeper reality of things. One may then enter through the threshold of Mystery. In *Prince Caspian*, especially in his beloved character Lucy Pevensie, C. S. Lewis turns quite deliberately to this sacramental metaphor of faith as seeing and the mystery that faith alone is able to apprehend.[19]

Indeed, Lucy's name is the first clue about her character.

In Christian hagiography, St. Lucy is the patron saint for those afflicted in the eyes. "Lucy" is etymologically derived from the Latin root *lucer*, which means "to shine." Christian tradition reports that the pagan nobleman who pursued St. Lucy loved her eyes so much that she tore them out saying, "Now let me live to God alone." St. Lucy's sight was miraculously restored; but her greater glory was in becoming a martyr, dying by the sword for refusing to renounce her faith in Christ.[20]

Memory and the Vision of Faith

Remembering (or memory) is a prominent theme in biblical religion that relates to faith's power to apprehend and to perceive. In Judaism and Christianity, faith (in its "seeing" and "grasping" modes) belongs within the context of a history of salvation. Remembrance of what God has done for us is an essential portion of the whole ongoing process of faith, that is, of perceiving, understanding, and responding with obedience to the will of God. Religious memory might be compared to the retina of the eye that captures the light and illuminates the object of sight. Only in the case of memory, the object of faith is itself the thing that is being illuminated. This is how spiritual vision comes into being.

We will not grasp wholly the meaning of faith as "seeing" and of how Lucy our heroine "saw," unless we understand this role of memory in relation to faith. Lewis sheds light on the matter in *Prince Caspian*. *Prince Caspian* is the story of how under the terribly adverse conditions of tyranny, a band of faithful Narnians continue to hold onto the memory of the central redemptive events in Narnia's past. This is when the great Lion Aslan, assisted by four sons and daughters of Adam, liberated Narnia from the wicked servitude of the White Witch. This memory is also the touchstone of hope for a future in which Narnia will be liberated from the present tyranny.

Lewis introduces the theme of remembering right at the start of the story. The four Pevensie children are waiting at a train station as they return to school from summer holiday. All at once they feel a strange pulling sensation. Edmund, the second youngest, exclaims: "Look sharp! . . . All catch hands together. This is magic—I can tell by the feeling. Quick!"[21] Then, suddenly, they are transported out of this world into a dense forest thicket in Narnia. At first the children do not recognize their surroundings. But they are hungry and thirsty, and so they set out in search of food and water. Their searching leads them to the ancient ruins of Cair Paravel, the castle in which they once reigned as kings and queens of Narnia. But they do not recognize it. Gradually, however, their hunger and the peculiar atmosphere of the surroundings help them to recall memories of long ago[22] Narnian adventures. Peter exclaims: "'Have none of you guessed where we are?' 'Go on, go on,' said Lucy. 'I've felt for hours that there was some wonderful mystery hanging over this place.' . . . 'We are in the ruins of Cair Paravel itself,' said Peter. . . . 'Don' t you *remember*?' (my emphasis here and in the following) . . . 'I do! I do!' said Lucy, and clapped her hands" (pp. 18–19). The children muster the courage to explore further. They uncover their coronation rings, jewelry, and armour. " 'Oh look! Our coronation rings—do you *remember* first wearing this?—Why, this is the little broach we all thought was lost—I say, isn't this the armour you wore in the great tournament in the Lone Islands?—Do you *remember* the Dwarf making that for me?—Do you *remember* drinking out of that horn?—Do you *remember*, do you *remember*?'" (p. 25).

Remembrance in Jewish and Christian faith often is expressed liturgically. I believe that these first scenes are liturgical and eucharistic. The dialogue rings with the musicality and rhythm of the ancient anaphoras (or thanksgiving) prayers of Jewish and Christian worship. The purpose of these prayers is to call to memory God and his gifts to the people and to offer thanksgiving (Gr. *eucharistia*). I do not think it is stretching things so far to say that even the hunger and the thirst that the children experience fit into a eucharistic scheme. The Christian eucharist takes place around a meal; and the children satisfy their hunger and thirst with repast and refreshment that sets them on a mission of redemption.

Seeing and the Gift of Presence

One doesn't read very far in *Prince Caspian* before it is evident that there are two principal heroes—Prince Caspian himself and little Lucy Pevensie. Each, in his and her own way, stands out as a character whose faith in the numinous figure of Aslan is severely tested. Each rises courageously to the occasion and as a result serves all of Narnia. The twentieth-century Protestant theologian Paul Tillich describes faith as "the self-affirmation of being in spite of fear and danger. The power of this self-affirmation," Tillich adds, "is the power of being which is effective in every act of courage." Thus faith may also be defined as "the experience of this power."[23] Both Prince Caspian and Lucy prove that they possess this power of faith and courage. It is with Lucy, however, that we will be concerned, and especially her gift of faith as "seeing" and how that contributes to the happy outcome of the story.

Lucy is the one who *sees*, as her name implies. She sees the fresh water stream and the apple trees near the castle ruins of Cair Paravel. She is the first to see the walls of the ruins. And when Peter challenges the children to guess where they are, Lucy responds: "Go on, go on, . . . I've felt for hours that there was some wonderful mystery hanging over this place" (pp. 18–19). But her physical sight and memory signify a more profound power of believing and seeing with the eyes of faith.

Nowhere is this power more dramatically portrayed than in two remarkably beautiful chapters: Chapter 9, "What Lucy Saw," and Chapter 10, "The Return of the Lion." In Chapter 9, the children and the dwarf Trumpkin (sent by Prince Caspian to try to locate the children) come ashore at evening onto the mainland, having cast off in a boat that morning from the island ruins of Cair Paravel. After dinner the entire party falls asleep, all, that is, except Lucy, whose wakefulness has a dreamlike quality under the moon and stars that bathe the water and the woods with the purest light. A nightingale sings, and as Lucy gazes up at the Narnian night sky, her memory is stirred. When Lucy's eyes have grown "accustomed to the light," she sees the trees "nearest her more distinctly," and a "great longing" washes over her "for the old days when the trees could talk in Narnia" (p. 122).

This scene is strongly reminiscent of Irene's journeys up to her grandmother's rooms. Lewis and MacDonald describe similar atmospheres as their respective heroines' consciousnesses are heightened and sharpened to the sense of a holy and numinous presence. Lewis probably reflects MacDonald's persuasion that when our "memory" of the numinous is awakened, *eros* will move the soul toward the object of its true desire. The "eyes" of the soul see even more deeply and clearly than the eyes of the body. Whereas our physical eyes may provide us with sensual delight, the soul's eyes are the receptors of real joy. In *Surprised by Joy*, his autobiographical essay, Lewis comments that this sort of joy breaks in upon the self like a wave of "unsatisfied desire which is itself more desirable than any other satisfaction . . . [and] anyone who has experienced it will want it again."[24]

At the start of *Prince Caspian*, after the children have quenched their thirst in the stream, Lucy remarks: "I do wish . . . , now that we're not thirsty, we could go on feeling as not-hungry as we did when we *were* thirsty" (p. 8). Lucy's hunger signifies a deeper desire to behold the transcendent. Although she does not yet realize it, Aslan is the true object of her desire. Joy is "a desire turned not to itself but to its object. Not only that, but it owes all its character to its object," writes Lewis.[25] Being awakened by joy is not the end of joy. Joy is "a road right out of the self" to its own object, he continues. This means not clinging to or identifying "with any object of the senses" but journeying to that which is "sheerly objective."[26] Nonetheless, we begin with the senses. So on that night Lucy turns to the trees and says, "Oh Trees, Trees, Trees . . . (though she had not been intending to speak at all). Oh Trees, wake, wake, wake. Don't you remember it? Don't you remember *me*? Dryads and Hamadryads, come out, come out, to me" (p. 123). For a moment it seems that the trees are going to come to life. "Though there was not a breath of wind they all stirred about her. . . . The nightingale stopped singing as if to listen to it. Lucy felt that at any moment she would begin to understand what the trees were trying to say. But the moment did not come. The rustling died away. The nightingale resumed its song. Even in the moonlight, the wood looked more ordinary again" (p. 123).

At this exact moment, Lucy experiences "a feeling (as you sometimes have when you are trying to remember a name or a date and almost get it, but it vanishes before you really do) that she had missed something: as if she had . . . used all the right words except one; or put in one word that was just wrong" (pp. 123–24). "Me" is the word misspoken ("Don't you remember *me*? . . . come out, to me"), and the word not spoken, the thought not thought, is Aslan. Aslan must try twice more before he is able to put Lucy on the right road out of herself.

The following day the Lion draws nearer. This is when the rescue party gets lost and is in danger of not reaching Prince Caspian in time to help. The children and Trumpkin arrive at a river gorge. They have been looking for the river Rush that they intend to follow to the Great River and the Fords of Beruna and straight on to Aslan's How (the ancient spot on which the great Stone Table once stood where Aslan was killed and was resurrected). The question is whether *this* river is the Rush, since in bygone days it did not run through a gorge. In which direction shall they go? Peter decides downstream. Then Lucy exclaims, "'Look! Look! Look! . . . The Lion . . . Aslan himself. Didn't you see?' Her face had changed completely and *her eyes shone*" (my emphasis) (p. 131). The others see nothing, however. They are all skeptical, all except Edmund, who betrayed Lucy in *The Lion, the Witch and Wardrobe* but was changed by his experiences in Narnia and the mercy that Aslan showed toward him. In desperation, Lucy insists that she has seen the Lion and that he wants them to go up the gorge rather than downstream. But her pleas do not persuade Peter and the others to change their direction. "So they set off to their right along the edge, downstream. And Lucy came last of the party, crying bitterly" (p. 134).

The decision to head downstream leads the party into an ambush by one of Miraz's scouting parties. They are forced now to turn around and retrace their steps back up the gorge. That evening they all enjoy a meal of freshly killed bear and apples. "It was a truly glorious meal. . . . Everyone felt quite hopeful now about finding King Caspian tomorrow and defeating Miraz in a few days" (p. 143). Afterward, everyone falls asleep and is not awakened, except Lucy. She wakes up "with the feeling that the voice she liked best in the world had been calling her name." And while Lucy cannot remember whose voice it is, nevertheless, "she was wonderfully rested and all the aches had gone from her bones—but because she felt so extremely happy and comfortable" (p. 144) she did not want to get up.

This scene is reminiscent of the scene in *The Princess and the Goblin* when Irene is bathed by her grandmother in the bottomless water of the mysterious silver basin. Like Irene in that scene, Lucy feels remarkably refreshed and spiritually regenerated. Whereas MacDonald uses the baptismal symbolism of water and light to mark an important change in Irene's character, Lewis returns to the eucharistic motifs of food and refreshment to signify an important change in Lucy's character.

"Awake, wider than anyone usually is" (p. 146), Lucy arises and walks among the trees. "And now there was no doubt that the trees were really moving—moving in and out through one another as if in a complicated country dance. . . . She went *fearlessly* (my emphasis) in among them, dancing herself," Lewis continues. "But she was only half interested in them. She wanted to get beyond them to something else; it was from beyond them that the dear voice had called." And in the midst of this dancing, "Oh, joy! For *he* was there: the huge Lion, shining white in the moonlight" (pp. 145, 146). The mystery is fulfilled in the real presence of the One who in Narnia is the object of every true and pure desire.

In a sermon, George MacDonald raises the following: "Do you ask, 'What is faith in him?' I answer, the leaving of your way, your objects, your self, and the taking of His and Him . . . *and doing as He tells you.* I can find no words strong enough to serve the weight of this necessity—this obedience."[27] C. S. Lewis included this passage among the 365 selections in his MacDonald anthology, and no doubt it left an impression on him, so much so that it became the inspiration for this scene.

Vision and Obedience: Lucy's True Test

Whatever the case, this appearance of Aslan in the moonlit forest is a stunning objective correlative of the gospel accounts of the Transfiguration of Jesus. The Reformed theologian Samuel Terrien describes the Transfiguration as an expression of the truth that "the vision of the glory [of God] cannot be divorced from the hearing of the voice."[28] What Lucy saw, soon the others would see as well. What Lucy heard, soon they would hear. They would see and they would hear because they too would be obedient. As MacDonald said elsewhere, "Obedience is the opener of the eyes"[29]

But the great Lion puts Lucy to her hardest test yet. She tries to excuse herself for failing the day before to persuade the others to follow him. How, she asks, was she to have followed him even if the others were unwilling? What would have been the outcome? Aslan's eyes tell Lucy he wants more from her. Then he speaks. "If you go back to the others now, and wake them up; and tell them you have seen me again; and that you must all get up at once and follow me—what will happen? There is only one way to find out" (p. 137). "A time comes to every man," wrote MacDonald, "when he must obey, or make such refusal—*and know it.*"[30] For Lucy that moment comes on this luminescent night.

> "Do you mean that is what you want me to do?" gasped Lucy.
>
> "Yes, little one," said Aslan.
>
> "Will the others see you too?"asked Lucy.
>
> "Certainly not at first," said Aslan. "Later on, it depends."
>
> "But they won't believe me!" said Lucy.
>
> "It doesn't matter," said Aslan.
>
> "Oh dear, oh dear," said Lucy. "And I was so pleased at finding you again. And I thought you'd let me stay. And I thought you'd come roaring in and frighten all the enemies away—like last time. And now everything is going to be horrid."
>
> "It is hard for you, little one," said Aslan. "But things never happen the same way twice."
>
> Lucy buried her head in his mane to hide from

his face. But there must have been magic in his mane. She could feel lion-strength going into her. Quite suddenly she sat up.

"I'm sorry, Aslan," she said. "I'm ready now."

"Now you are a lioness," said Aslan. "And now all Narnia will be renewed." (p. 150)

This marvelous scene and the accompanying dialogue really require no further commentary. Lucy is no longer the child she once was. In a short time she has grown up to achieve the moral and spiritual stature of a true heroine of faith and courage. She is the first to see and hear Aslan because her yearning for him is the strongest and the purest. Terrien says: "In biblical faith, presence eludes, but does not delude. The hearing of the name, which is obedience to the will and the decision to live now for an eternal future, becomes the proleptic vision of the glory."[31] What Lucy failed to do in the first instance she does not fail to do this time. This time she obeys completely and follows the great Lion. And the others follow her, even though at first they do not see or hear Aslan. "She fixed her eyes on Aslan. He turned and walked at a slow pace about thirty yards ahead of them. The others had only Lucy's direction to guide them, for Aslan was not only invisible to them but silent as well" (pp. 157–58).

John Henry Newman says in one of his Oxford Sermons: "Every act of obedience is an approach—an approach to Him who is not far off, though he seems so, but close behind the invisible screen of things which hides Him from us. . . . You have to seek his face; obedience is the only way of seeing Him."[32] Through obedience, Peter, Susan, and Edmund, and even the skeptic

Trumpkin, eventually catch sight of Aslan and hear his roar. And with that roar Aslan awakens all of the sleeping land and seals the triumph of goodness over evil in Narnia.

The Vision of God and the Kingdom

C. S. Lewis's sensibilities, no doubt, were less mystical than George MacDonald's. But he too draws the important connections between faith and courage enacted as moral character and faith and courage fulfilled in the vision of God. Lewis depicts this final fulfillment of faith and courage with moving effect in the seventh, concluding book of the Narnia series. The story of *The Last Battle* recounts the final days of the Narnian world when wickedness conspires against goodness and wins the temporal struggle. Nevertheless, even in these latter days as evil stalks the land, Narnia is not without noble and courageous defenders who are faithful to the ancient truth and the good name of Aslan. Nor does Aslan abandon this faithful remnant.

As King Tirian, the last, noble king of Narnia, is taken down in battle, a miraculous event occurs behind the doorway of a mysterious stable. In the final moment of his life, Tirian is forced through the doorway of that stable and beholds within, not the interior of a stable, but a whole fresh new world. Now standing before him are fourteen kings and queens, those heroes and heroines from our world who had been transported to Narnia at critical moments in its history and by their noble deeds ensured that goodness and right reigned there—all friends of Aslan, and Lucy is among them.

It would take too long to explain the exact circumstances of this occurrence. I leave that for the reader to discover. What is of immediate importance is the fact that every one of these heroes and heroines of Narnia is now on the other side of death. All have met their temporal end, whether in Narnia or in England, including three of the Pevensie children, all except Susan, in a train wreck. As Aslan says, they are now in the "Shadowlands—dead. The term is over: the holidays have begun. The dream is ended: this is the morning."[33] In the conversations that follow, Lucy is given to speak and raise questions and make observations much as she always has. But I think that in her speech Lewis also supplies the last important key that unlocks the lineage and legacy of her remarkable character.

Lucy literally utters a litany of observations that clarify just where everyone is. With the help of her sharp eyes and extraordinary powers of perception, the whole company is able to identify the familiar and yet transformed landscape that surrounds them. They realize that they are in a new Narnia, an archetype and perfection of that world whose ending they just witnessed. And they are drawn in (or is it out?) toward the places of their deepest love and desire, only these places are more beautiful now than they ever were before. Finally, everyone arrives at the walls of a garden, a place familiar to some among the party who once upon a time visited a garden very much like this one when Narnia was fresh in creation. They see before them a panorama within the garden walls which is somehow even larger and greater than the country outside.

Lucy speaks once again:

> "I *see* (my emphasis throughout)," she said at last, thoughtfully. "I *see* now. This garden is like the Stable.

> It is far bigger inside than outside." . . .
>
> Lucy looked hard at the garden and *saw* that it was not really a garden at all but a whole world, with its own rivers and woods and sea and mountains. But they were not strange: she knew them all.
>
> 'I *see*," she said. "This is still Narnia, and, more real, and more beautiful than the Narnia down below, just as *it* was more real and more beautiful than the Narnia outside the Stable door! I *see* . . . world within world, Narnia within Narnia." (pp. 224–25)

We should take note especially of the repetitive and responsive quality of Lucy's speech. The whole of it is musical, liturgical, and celebrative. She ends her speech with this exclamatory phrasing: "I see . . . world within world, Narnia within Narnia," which I take to be a deliberate variation on the ancient liturgical formula, "Now and forever and to the ages of ages. Amen."

Through Lucy's special eyes we see the new and eternal Narnia. "Lucy looked this way and that and soon found that a new beautiful thing had happened to her. Whatever she looked at, however far away it might be, once she had fixed her eyes steadily on it, it became quite clear and close as if she were looking through a telescope." Lucy's eyes see so far and with such sharpness that she makes out in the far distance something that, although it first appears to be "a brightly-colored cloud"; is "a real land." She points this out to Edmund and Peter, and together they recognize that the land that lies in front of them is England. Then they catch sight of "Professor Kirke's old home in the country" where, through the mysterious wardrobe, their journeys to Narnia began; and they are puzzled. This is because the home had been destroyed some years ago. However, their old Narnian friend Mr. Tumnus, the faun, tells them that what they are seeing is "the England within England, the real England just as real as the real Narnia. And in that inner England no good thing is destroyed" (p. 226).

And if you or I ask how come the others are now able to see what Lucy sees, the answer is that "their eyes also had become like hers" (p. 226). Eyes of true faith are rewarded with the vision of God. Then fear is also ended, courage is completed, and every worthy desire is joyfully fulfilled. "Aslan turned to them and said: 'You do not yet look so happy as I mean you to be.' Lucy said, 'We're afraid of being sent way, Aslan. And you have sent us back in our own world so often.' 'No fear of that,' said Aslan. 'Have you not guessed?' Their hearts leaped and a wild hope rose within them" (pp. 227–28).

Aslan tells Lucy, Edmund, Peter, and the others who were with them at the train station what they have already suspected, that they were killed in a real railway accident. But now they have passed beyond the "Shadow-lands" where it is always "the morning." As Aslan explained these things, they all *saw* more than they had ever seen before. And Aslan "no longer looked to them like a lion; but the things that began to happen after that," says Lewis, "were so great and beautiful that I cannot write them" (p. 228).

Conclusion
A Bibliographical Essay

In the poem *East Coker,* T. S. Eliot says that "old men ought to be explorers." And as I am about to turn fifty years of age, I appreciate more than ever this bit of the poet's wisdom. Of course Eliot is employing a metaphor. He does not mean that octogenarians ought to go on a voyage across vast seas as Magellan or Columbus or traverse great continents like Marco Polo. He does mean, however, that the moral and spiritual truths that make us fully human are not so much objects that we hold as visions beheld and constantly striven for. We envision truth and it captures our whole being and draws us constantly forward "Into another intensity? / For a further union, a deeper communion."

When Eliot implores that "old men ought to be explorers" he also suggests that in a mysterious way "in my beginning is my end" and that "in my end is my beginning." In order for us to be true "seafarers" and "explorers" in old age, we must begin learning and practicing the skills of virtuous living in our youth. Our children cannot learn these skills on their own. The moral imagination needs to be cultivated like the tea rose in a garden. Left unattended and unfed, the rose will languish and thistle will grow in its place.

Throughout this book I have done my best to demonstrate how fairy tales feed the moral imagination with the best food. There is no single solution to the moral crisis of childhood in our culture. But that something is seriously awry few would deny. Gilbert Meilaender writes that "if Plato is correct, if we cannot insert vision into the blind and our environment shapes our perceptions and judgments of goodness, one whose vision of the good is not properly shaped in childhood may never come to see—except perhaps by 'divine intervention.'"[1] We are at a point in many Western societies where Plato's admonition points straight at us. Our children are in jeopardy and so is the future of virtue and human goodness as well.

The people who attend my adult education classes come from every economic station and every racial, ethnic, and religious background. But they all agree that our children are in jeopardy. As a black comic quipped one evening on *Showtime at the Apollo*—my daughter Victoria's favorite television show: "Now there isn't anything wrong with our children. But there is something the matter with the way we are raising them."

Our concern for our children brings us together. The parents, teachers, pastors, and rabbis whom I teach want something better for our children and are tired of hearing lamentation and excuses. They want to do something themselves. Reading good stories to our children is one small way to begin—and everyone can do it. But my greatest frustration in writing this book is that for the sake of economy and clarity I have had to select only a few of the stories that my children and I have read together and that have been the staple of my classroom teaching. So in the next few pages let me take the opportunity to pass on the titles of some more of my favorite stories. I have ordered my discussion along the lines of the topics in the chapters of this book.

Becoming Real

Stories about "Becoming Real" (or transformation) abound in the fairy-tale and fantasy genres. But I will mention just three that I love best: "The Ugly Duckling," *Where the Wild Things Are,* and "Rocking-Horse Land."

Hans Christian Andersen's "The Ugly Duckling" is a masterpiece that, like so many of his stories, also contains searing social criticism and profound insights into human nature and conduct. Adults will read this story with grown-up interest. Nonetheless, "The Ugly Duckling" is a story that captivates children because it is also *about* growing up. So often "The Ugly Duckling" is valued for the lesson it teaches about misjudging others by their appearance. And no doubt the story lends itself to this interpretation. When we read "The Ugly Duckling" in this way, however, our attention shifts from the ugly duckling to those who make fun of him, ridicule him, and dismiss him from their company. We begin to see the ugly duckling as a stereotypical passive victim of social prejudice. But the ugly duckling is not a victim and he is not passive: he is a survivor and a victor.

In the end, the ugly duckling is transformed into a beautiful swan like those he has admired and only dreamed he might become. It is easy to regard this transformation as just the inevitable or predestined outcome of his genetic constitution and that he does not control or determine who or what he becomes. In a literal sense, this might be true: the ugly duckling never was a duck and always was a swan. However, let me suggest that the important interest of the story is about how the ugly duckling *acts* independently to become who he is in the end. At the beginning of the story, he leaves his "family" and goes out in the "wide world" to escape ridicule and ostracism. Yet this also commences a difficult journey that tests his character and makes him every bit as strong and noble and good and beautiful inside as he eventually becomes on the outside. Like the velveteen rabbit, the ugly duckling deals with the ridicule of his own kind, and like the little mermaid he resists the temptation to grow bitter, jealous, and resentful.

Maurice Sendak's *Where the Wild Things Are* is one of the most popular children's stories of our generation. And while I have avoided discussing the genre of children's picture books, I could not let pass the opportunity to add my voice to the chorus of praise and love for this story. With its wonderful illustrations and crisp text, *Where the Wild Things Are* achieves brilliance in its simplicity. It is a story about learning to discipline one's passions and one's appetites lest one become a beast, one of the "wild things." It is about the difficult task of training one's imagination. And it teaches the important lesson that every child needs both the discipline and the love of his or her parents in order to become a true son or daughter and to become wholly human.

The last story under this topic of becoming real is Laurence Houseman's "Rocking-Horse Land." This story shares much in common with *The Velveteen Rabbit* insofar as it is built around the relationship of a child with his toy. Prince Fredolin's love of his rocking-horse makes the wooden horse come alive. The young prince releases his friend from the nursery to join forever the real and alive horses in Rocking-Horse Land. The story also teaches an important lesson about friendship: we must always respect the freedom of a friend, for absent that respect, true friendship cannot survive nor do we grow to become mature persons.

Love and Immortality

"Snow White and the Seven Dwarfs ("Snow-drop") by Jacob and Wilhelm Grimm ranks among the best and the most beloved of fairy tales. But first we must get out of our minds the Disney version. As in so many cases, Disney has turned this popular fairy tale into a story about romantic love. There is hardly a hint of that in the Grimm's story.

It is said that our going to sleep at night and arising in the morning is a rehearsal for our death and awakening to immortality. And so it seems to me also that this is the deep intuition on which this story is built. Because they love her so much the seven dwarfs do everything within their power to prevent the worst to become of Snow White at the hands of her wicked stepmother. Nor do they stop loving her even in "death." For three symbolic days, "all seven watched and bewailed" Snow White's fall into the deep sleep that they feared was death. But "because her cheeks remained rosy, and her face looked just as it did when she was alive," they did not bury her in "the cold earth" but placed her in a "coffin of glass." The dwarfs continue to hope for Snow White's awakening, until the day a prince comes who falls in love with her at first sight and whose kiss brings her back to life.

George MacDonald wrote a precious and beautiful little story that has also been published in lovely picture book versions. "Little Daylight" is based on the "Sleeping Beauty" story and contains important elements of "Snow White" and "Beauty and the Beast" as well. It concerns a young princess who at her christening has a curse imposed on her by an evil fairy. She is condemned to sleep during the day and to arise at night when her vitality is decided by the waxing and waning of the moon. Finally, a young prince discovers her and breaks the spell. One night when the moon has waned, he finds the princess. She appears as an old woman and the prince does not recognize that she is the young maiden with whom he has fallen in love. Nevertheless, he pities the old woman whom he thinks is dying, and kisses her on the lips. Then she stands up transformed into Little Daylight. And she says to him, "You kissed me when I was an old woman: there! I kiss you when I am a young princess—Is the sun coming?" I think this is one of the most beautiful and moving of all fairy-tale stories.

A third favorite under this topic of love and immortality is Oscar Wilde's masterfully told story of "The Selfish Giant." It can be read at many levels and is so appealing to the young because it is about the role that children play in helping a great Giant to repent of his selfishness and give his beloved garden over to them to play in. I shall leave the allegory and biblical allusions for you to find.

George MacDonald's *The Golden Key* is a far more

difficult and complex story than the three I have mentioned. It is symbolic and allegorical. The story is about the mysterious journeys of a young girl and boy. They are joined, then separated, and finally reunited in a place where the rainbow ends, beyond the earth in "the country whence the shadows fall." I read this story for the first time one evening to my son Rafi when he was eight or nine. Rafi fell asleep, but I did not notice. I must have gone on for an hour and a half. I lost track of time. I was completely enthralled by the pictures MacDonald was painting with his words and the mood and atmosphere of the story. Rafi was probably too young for this story. I don't know whether one is ever ready for it. It is a personal favorite, though it is probably not for everyone.

Friends and Mentors

Kenneth Grahame's humorous tale of *The Reluctant Dragon* gives us the most endearing dragon in all of children's literature, and a mentor to a young boy to boot. This dragon is a fellow who much prefers poetry and good conversation to pillaging or destruction. He befriends the boy and teaches him about loyalty and trust and the responsibilities of friendship. A dragon may seem to be the most unlikely of mentors. Yet here is one such dragon.

As much as I like E. B. White's story of *Charlotte's Web*, I personally have enjoyed another of his three children's books even more—*The Trumpet of the Swan*. I admit that this may have to do with the fact that it is a boy's adventure, as young Sam Beaver finds and befriends a trumpeter swan who is without a voice. Much humor and good fun is built on this premise. But most of all, this is a story about friendships and how they can help us to succeed in life and become better persons in the process. The character of Louis the young trumpeter swan is unforgettable for his sincerity, integrity, and sheer joy in living.

The story of "Damon and Pythias" is not a fairy tale or modern fantasy story. But I could not finish this section without mentioning it. It is the classical tale of two friends from the ancient city of Syracuse. The lesson of "Damon and Pythias" approximates the biblical saying that there is no greater love that a man can give than to lay down his life for a friend. Damon may not lay down his life for his friend Pythias, but he is willing to do so. And Pythias would do no less than to use his last bit of strength to keep his promise to Damon so that Damon might live. Happily, William J. Bennett has included this story in *The Book of Virtues*.

Evil and Redemption

Fairy tales and children's fantasy stories almost inevitably present us with good characters who struggle against evil or find evil in their path or have to learn how to know when evil is present, when to avoid it, and when to meet it head on. But I am restricting this discussion to just two stories.

The Victorian writer John Ruskin's *The King of the Golden River* is a masterpiece of storytelling. It is rich in ethical themes and contemporary in the attention it gives to such social concerns as child abuse, alcohol (and drug) addiction, and respect for the environment. But Ruskin avoids didacticism almost entirely. His is pure storytelling that reads like a biblical parable. Indeed, one could argue that in the background of *The King of the*

Golden River are at least two biblical parables: the stories from the Gospel of Luke of the Good Samaritan and the beggar Lazarus and the Rich Man. In any case, the principal characters of Ruskin's tale are three brothers; the two older brothers named Schwartz and Hans are cruel and greedy and the youngest named Gluck is kind and generous. And there is of course also the gnomelike and very mysterious King of the Golden River.

The other story I want to mention is the last book in C. S. Lewis's Narnia series. *The Last Battle* is the story of the final days of Narnia. But ultimately it is not a dark tale. Even though evil seems to win out, heroism, goodness, and truth do find their reward in an eternal Narnia in which what is real is more vivid and beautiful than anything in the old Narnia. In this book Lewis manages also to teach a powerful lesson about how wretched selfishness and falsehood really are and to present a compelling vision of death that transcends tragedy.

Heroines (and Heroes) of Faith and Courage

In Chapter 6 I discussed the first of George MacDonald's Curdie and Irene stories, *The Princess and the Goblin*. In the sequel, *Curdie and the Princess*, Curdie is sent on a mission by the mysterious grandmother to save Irene and her father the king from a vicious plot that threatens the kingdom. Not only is Curdie's faith tested but his native courage and wit are called upon in such a way that he truly grows up. In the first half of the book, especially, MacDonald teaches some wonderful lessons about character and vision. If we are ugly inside, then virtue and goodness themselves look ugly or threatening to us. If we are obedient, trusting, and virtuous, we gain a special capacity to distinguish good from evil, even when evil hides beneath deceptive covers.

L. Frank Baum's *The Wonderful Wizard of Oz* (and its sequels) and Madeleine L'Engle's *A Wrinkle in Time* (and its sequels) are far better known to contemporary parents and children. Little needs to be said about these two stories. In the first case, the book really deserves to be read, in spite of the great attraction and success of the movie with Judy Garland. My students know and like *The Wrinkle in Time* almost as well as *Charlotte's Web.* I have often juxtaposed this story and its young heroine, Meg, with the stories and characters I have discussed in Chapter 6. Meg, Irene, and Lucy are heroines every young girl should meet. Meg, of course, is called upon to outgrow her early adolescent insecurities and trust in herself and her good mentors from other planets in order to rescue her brother and father from captivity under a cosmic power of darkness personified as the *It.* Thus, I may well have included this story also under the topic of evil and redemption. For it truly is built upon that theme.

In closing, I want to mention several anthologies that contain many of the shorter stories that I have discussed. I recommend the following: *The Victorian Fairy Tale Book,* ed. Michael Patrick Hearn (Pantheon Books, 1988); *The Classic Fairy Tales*, eds. Ionia and Peter Opie (Oxford University Press, 1980); *The Oxford Book of Modern Fairy Tales*, ed. Alison Lurie (Oxford University Press, 1993); and *The Book of Virtues,* William J. Bennett (Simon and Schuster, 1993).

Notes

Introduction

1. C. S. Lewis, *The Abolition of Man* (New York: Collier Books/Macmillan Publishing Co., 1947), p.35.

2. Bruno Bettelheim, *The Uses of Enchantment* (New York: Alfred A. Knopf, 1975), p. 5.

3. William J. Bennett, ed., *The Book of Virtues* (New York: Simon and Schuster, 1993).

4. In addition there is a large body of work on traditional fairy tales. Virtually all of it, however, is strongly influenced by structuralism where there is little appreciation for the moral content of the stories.

5. C. S. Lewis, *Of Other Worlds*, ed. Walter Hooper (New York: Harcourt Brace Javanovich, 1975), p. 24.

6. Gilbert K. Chesterson, *Lunacy and Letters,* ed. Dorothy Collins (London and New York: Sheed and Ward, 1958), p. 107.

7. Gilbert. K. Chesterton, *Orthodoxy* (Garden City, N.Y.: Image Books, Doubleday and Co., 1959), p. 60.

Chapter 1

1. Flannery O'Connor, *Mystery and Manners* (New York: Farrar, Straus and Giroux, 1990), p. 96.

2. Alasdair MacIntyre, *After Virtue: A Study in Moral Theory,* 2d ed. (Notre Dame, Ind.: University of Notre Dame Press, 1984), p. 216.

3. Gilbert. K. Chesterton, *Orthodoxy* (Garden City, N.Y.: Image Books, Doubleday and Co., 1959), p. 50.

4. Chesterton, *Orthodoxy,* p. 52.

5. Martin Buber, *Between Man and Man* (New York: Macmillan, 1978), p. 105.

6. Ionia and Peter Opie, eds., *The Classic Fairy Tales* (New York: Oxford University Press, 1980), pp. 182–83. This is the English translation of Madame de Beaumont's version of the fairy tale published originally in French in 1756, subsequently translated into English in 1761.

7. Gertrude Himmelfarb, *The Demoralization of Society: From Victorian Virtues to Modern Values* (New York: Alfred A. Knopf, 1995), p. 10.

8. Himmelfarb, *The Demoralization of Society,* p. 11.

9. These are collected in Gilbert K. Chesterton, *What's Wrong with the World* (New York: Dodd, Mead and Co., 1910).

10. Chesterton, *What's Wrong with the World,* p. 252–53.

11. Chesterton, *What's Wrong with the World,* p. 254.

12. Chesterton, *What's Wrong with the World,* p. 253.

13. Chesterton, *Orthodoxy,* p. 59.

Chapter 2

1. Maurice Sendak, *Caldecott & Co.: Notes on Books and Culture* (New York: Noonday Press, 1990), p. 114.

2. Sendak, *Caldecott & Co.*, p. 113.

3. Sendak, *Caldecott & Co.*, p. 115.

4. Carlo Collodi, *Pinocchio*, trans. E. Harden (New York: Puffin Books, Viking Penguin, 1974), p. 132. All subsequent page references to this edition will be made parenthetically in the text.

5. C. S. Lewis, *Mere Christianity* (New York: Macmillan, 1960), p. 154.

6. Lewis, *Mere Christianity*, p. 154.

7. Sendak, *Caldecott & Co.* , p. 113.

8. Josef Pieper, *A Brief Reader of the Virtues of the Human Heart,* trans. Paul C. Duggan (San Francisco: Ignatius Press, 1991), p. 21.

9. Josef Pieper, *Josef Pieper: An Anthology* (San Francisco, Ignatius Press, 1989), p. 53.

10. I am citing here the less readily available critical English edition done by Nicholas J. Perella, trans., *The Adventures of Pinocchio: Story of a Puppet* (Berkeley: University of California Press, 1986), p.

427. I have used this edition where the other standard editions have left out phrases or sentences—often pious expressions or religious references—that are, nevertheless, essential to our understanding of the story.

11. *The Confessions,* trans. R. S. Pine-Coffin (New York: Penguin Books, 1961), p. 92 (Bk 5: 2).

12. Perella, trans., *The Adventures of Pinocchio*, p. 443.

13. Pieper, *A Brief Reader on the Virtues of the Human Heart*, p. 25.

14. Pieper, *A Brief Reader on the Virtues of the Human Heart*, pp. 25–26.

15. C. S. Lewis, *Prince Caspian* (New York: HarperCollins, 1994), p. 128. I have decided to use the 1994 HarperCollins edition of the Narnia books. It replaces the popular Macmillan Collier Books printing, 1970, which is now no longer available. Because of redesign, the page numbering differs in the new HarperCollins printing. This applies also to my citations from *Prince Caspian, The Last Battle*, and *The Lion, the Witch and the Wardrobe* in chapters 5 and 6.

16. In June 1994, the "Colloquium on Everyday Ethics" held at the Institute on Religion and Public Life discussed *Pinocchio*. The papers written for that occasion and the discussions that ensued have contributed to this essay. I here want to acknowledge my indebtedness to that forum and the insights of my colleagues.

Chapter 3

1. Robert Coles, *The Spiritual Life of Children* (Boston: Houghton Mifflin, 1990), p. 37.

2. Margery Williams, *The Velveteen Rabbit* (New York: Simon and Schuster, 1983). The text is not paginated.

3. While Williams's story has found its way into nurseries and playrooms for several generations, it is also being used in nursing homes and care centers for the elderly. Students in adult night school courses who work in health and psychiatric care settings have reported that *The Velveteen Rabbit* is a comfort to the old and the infirm. How the Skin Horse and the Velveteen Rabbit become real is like what it is to grow old and still have dignity and worth.

4. Martin Buber, *I and Thou,* 2nd ed. (New York: Charles Scribner's Sons, 1958), p. 11.

5. Roger Sale, *Fairy Tales and After: From Snow White to E. B. White* (Cambridge, Mass.: Harvard University Press, 1978), chap. 3.

6. Sale, *Fairy Tales*, p. 67.

7. Jack Zipes, *Fairy Tales and the Art of Subversion* (New York: Routledge, 1991), p. 85.

8. I have used L. W. Kingsland's translation of *The Little Mermaid* in *Hans Andersen's Fairy Tales: A Selection*, World's Classics (New York: Oxford University Press, 1984), p. 79. Subsequent page references to the story will be made parenthetically in the text.

9. C. S. Lewis, *Letters to Malcolm* (New York: Harcourt Brace Javanovich, 1964), p. 121.

10. G. K. Chesterton, *Orthodoxy* (Garden City, N. Y.: Image Books/Doubleday and Company, 1959), p. 102.

11. I am going to pass up the opportunity to pursue the conjecture that there is an allusion here to a young woman's menstrual cycle. That frankly does not interest me so much as the fact that allusions to blood and the color red abound in this story which unmistakably suggest the sacral and redemptive meaning of the same.

12. Sale, *Fairy Tales*, p. 67.

13. Peter Kreeft, *Heaven: The Heart's Deepest Longing* (San Francisco: Harper and Row, 1980), p. 65.

14. Kreeft, *Heaven*, p. 63.

15. See, especially, the story told in 1 Sam. 26.

Chapter 4

1. Aristotle, *Nicomachean Ethics,* in *The Basic Works of Aristotle*, ed. Richard McKeon (New York: Random House, 1941), p. 1058 (Bk. 8).

2. *Nicomachean Ethics*, p. 1088.

3. Kenneth Grahame, *The Wind in the Willows* (New York: Signet Classic, 1969), p. 27. Subsequent references to the book will be made parenthetically in the text.

4. *Nicomachean Ethics*, p. 1058.

5. E. B. White, *Charlotte's Web* (New York: Harper and Row, 1952), p. 165. Subsequent references to the book will be made parenthetically in the text.

6. *Nicomachean Ethics*, pp. 1065–1066.

7. Lest there be a misunderstanding, even in the purer sort of mentoral relationship, the formation of that relationship is not merely unilateral. The student or mentee will desire to study under the mentor and may take the initiative of proposal. However, the mentor decides whether the mentoral relationship will be formed.

8. Felix Salten, *Bambi: A Life in the Woods,* trans. Whittaker Chambers (New York: A Minstrel Book, 1988), p. 57. Subsequent references to the book will be made parenthetically in the text.

Chapter 5

1. I have used the translation of *The Snow Queen* in L. W. Kingsland, *Hans Andersen's Fairy Tales: A Selection,* Worlds' Classics (New York: Oxford University Press, 1984), p. 229 Subsequent page references to the story will be made parenthetically within the text.

2. Paul Evdokimov, *The Struggle with God* (Glen Rock, N.J.: Paulist Press, 1966), p. 78.

3. See, for example, Wolfgang Lederer's book-length study titled *The Kiss of the Snow Queen* (Berkeley: University of California Press, 1986); especially on Kay's changed behavior, see pp. 23–28.

4. "Unlike his father, who was an atheist, Andersen was a deeply religious person, whose religious beliefs may be summed up by saying that he believed in the existence of a god, in the importance of behaving decently, and the immortality of the soul. This famous triad of God, Virtue and Immortality, which is the basis of theological rationalism, was also the basis of Andersen's religious belief. . . . Andersen's religion was a primitive and undogmatic one, in which he saw Christ as the great teacher and model to mankind, and Nature as God's universal church." Elias Bredsdorff, *Hans Christian Andersen* (New York: Charles Scribner's Sons, 1975), pp. 297–98. Nevertheless, it needs to be said also that Andersen's religious sensibilities outpaced any sort of simple theological rationalism. There was the mystic in him as well.

5. Nicholas Berdyaev, *The Destiny of Man* (New York: Harper and Row, 1960), p. 23.

6. Lederer, *Kiss of the Snow Queen,* p. 183.

7. Kathryn Lindskoog, *The Lion of Judah in Never-Never Land* (Grand Rapids, Mich.: Wm. B. Eerdmans, 1973), pp. 96–97.

8. Evan K. Gibson, *C. S. Lewis: Spinner of Tales* (Washington D.C.: Christian University Press, 1980), p. 136.

9. C. S. Lewis, *The Lion, the Witch and the Wardrobe,* Harper Trophy Book, (New York: HarperCollins, 1994), p. 34. See also chapter 2, note 15 in this book.

10. Lindskoog, *Lion of Judah,* p. 96.

11. Gilbert Meilaender, *The Taste for the Other: The Social and Ethical Thought of C. S. Lewis* (Grand Rapids, Mich.: Wm. B.

Eerdmans, 1978), p. 9.

12. Gibson, *C. S. Lewis: Spinner of Tales,* (p. 141).

Chapter 6

1. From *A Dish of Orts*, quoted by Roderick McGillis in his Introduction to George MacDonald, *The Princess and the Goblin, The Princess and Curdie*, also ed. by Roderick McGillis (New York: Oxford University Press, 1990), p. xxii. Subsequent page references to this volume will be made parenthetically in the text.

2. This scene is suspiciously reminiscent of Lewis Carroll's *Alice's Adventures in Wonderland* (1865)—that was published seven years earlier. MacDonald and Carroll were close friends. Carroll's sequel *Through the Looking Glass* was published in the same year as *The Princess and the Goblin*, 1872.

3. See, for example, Nancy-Lou Patterson, "*Kore* Motifs in the *Princess and the Goblin*, in *For the Childlike*, ed. Roderick McGillis (Meteuchen, N.J.: The Children's Literature Association and the Scarecrow Press, 1992), pp. 169–82. Patterson also mentions that the spinning wheel and thread being spun are motifs associated with the virgin goddess Athena and the Three Fates of classical Greco-Roman mythology. But these motifs are also associated with Mary in iconography of the Annunciation. A contemporary of MacDonald in England, Dante Gabriel Rossetti experimented with these and other motifs that we find in MacDonald's story. In his painting *Ecce Ancilla Domini* ("Behold the Handmaid of the Lord"), completed in 1849–50, Rossetti tried to invent a new iconography. In this Annunciation setting, he placed a hand loom at the foot of Mary's bed and a soft blue curtain behind Mary's head, the latter suggesting the ideals of truth and spiritual love. The loom is a loom of life on which is spun the loftiest dreams, or perhaps this is the traditional symbolism of the new life that she will gestate in her womb.

4. The descriptive passages cited in the paragraph are especially reminiscent of Revelation 12:1–2 NEB: "After that there appeared a great sign in heaven: a woman robed with the sun, beneath her feet the moon and on her head a crown of twelve stars. She was about to bear a child, and in the anguish of her labour she cried out to be delivered." In the Christian church this passage with its clear allusions to Israel and the twelve tribes has also been interpreted as a vision or sign of Mary. There are other reasons to suspect that MacDonald was employing symbolism through which he intended to suggest the Virgin Mary. In Christian art and liter-

ature the moon also has often stood for Mary the Mother of God *who* reflects the light of the Son. A comparison with Dante Gabriel Rossetti's poem "The Blessed Damsel" is also interesting in this regard.

5. See the Patterson essay (note 3 above) and others in *For the Childlike.*

6. MacDonald, *The Princess and the Goblin, The Princess and Curdie,* n. 5, pp. 343–44.

7. *Macmillan School Dictionary,* 3rd ed., S.V. "courage."

8. George MacDonald, *Creation in Christ,* from the Unspoken Sermons, ed. Rolland Hein (Wheaton, Ill.: Harold Shaw Publishers, 1976), p. 84 (Sermon: "The Fear of God").

9. MacDonald, *Creation in Christ,* p. 199 (Sermon: "Life").

10. MacDonald, *Creation in Christ,* pp. 199–200 (Sermon: "Life").

11. MacDonald tells two intertwining stories of faith and courage in *The Princess and the Goblin.* One is Princess Irene's story and the other is Curdie's. MacDonald once wrote that "doubts are the messengers of the Living One to the honest. They are the first knock at our door of things, that are not yet but have to be understood. . . . Doubt must precede every deeper assurance, for uncertainties are what we first see when we look into a region hitherto unknown." C. S. Lewis, ed., *George MacDonald: An Anthology* (New York: Simon and Schuster, 1996), pp. 66–67. This is how Curdie's own journey to faith goes. Finally, he does join those others in the story (including his own mother) for whom the grandmother and the transcendent and beneficent reality she represents are profoundly real and a source of hope and courage.

12. Josef Pieper, *The Four Cardinal Virtues* (New York: Harcourt, Brace and World, 1965), p. 140.

13. MacDonald, *Creation in Christ,* p. 282 (Sermon: "Self Denial").

14. Pieper, *Four Cardinal Virtues,* p. 140.

15. Madconald, *Creation in Christ,* p. 161 (Sermon: "The Consuming Fire").

16. Lewis, ed., *George MacDonald,* p. xxxiii.

17. Lewis, ed. *George MacDonald,* p. xxxiv.

18. Lewis, ed. *George MacDonald,* p. 18.

19. Both MacDonald and Lewis are clear in their conviction that while God, in his infinite being, transcends the words and images through which human beings express and try to make sense of their experience of his self-revelation to them, neverthe-

less, God uses the imaginative and metaphor-making capacities of human beings to bridge the ontological gap that separates creature and Creator. Both MacDonald and Lewis propose powerful sacramental visions of creation. In this sacramental understanding, all creaturely things, including our metaphors of speech, may become windows through which we "see" the Uncreated. Even our physical capacity of sight is a sign and symbol of another capacity of spiritual vision. And while this spiritual capacity has been severely debilitated by sin, faith may remedy the affliction. Thus, through faith's "eyes" we may behold once more the Creative Will behind all things.

20. E. Cobham Brewer, *Dictionary of Phrase and Fable*, 17th ed., revised (Philadelphia: J. B. Lippincott and Co., n.d.), p. 530.

21. C. S. Lewis, *Prince Caspian,* Harper Trophy (New York: HarperCollins, 1994), p.3. Subsequent page references will appear parenthetically in the text.

22. Long ago by Narnian chronology; only several months ago by our (earth's) time.

23. Paul Tillich, *The Courage to Be* (New Haven: Yale University Press, 1952), p. 172.

24. Lewis, *Surprised by Joy* (New York: Harcourt Brace Jovanovich, 1955), pp. 17–18.

25. Lewis, *Surprised*, p. 220.

26. Lewis, *Surprised*, p. 221.

27. MacDonald, *Creation in Christ*, p. 98 (Sermon: "The Truth in Jesus").

28. Samuel Terrien, *The Elusive Presence* (San Francisco: Harper and Row, 1978), p. 426.

29. Lewis, ed., *George MacDonald,* p. 28.

30. MacDonald, *Creation in Christ*, p. 115 (Sermon: "The Way").

31. Terrien, *Elusive Presence,* pp. 476–77.

32. John Henry Newman, *Miscellanies: From the Oxford Sermons and Other Writings* (London: Strahan and Co., 1870), p. 323 (from the sermon "Watching").

33. C. S. Lewis, *The Last Battle,* Harper Trophy (New York: HarperCollins, 1994), p. 228.

Conclusion

1. Gibert C. Meilaender, *The Theory and Practice of Virtue* (Notre Dame, Ind.: University of Notre Dame Press, 1984), p. 54.

Index